*new york's
50+ best
little
shops

*By Ranjani
Gopalarathinam*

universe publishing

Acknowledgments

I'd like to thank my sister, Nandini, for letting me draw upon her vast vocabulary of clothing and fashion in writing this book, my parents, Leslie Falk for presenting me with this opportunity, my savvy, stupendous friends who shed light on so many of the nooks in the city this book takes you to, and all the fantastic people who are building the vivid tapestry of the New York City marketplace.

First published in the United States of America in 2005
by Universe Publishing
a division of Rizzoli International Publications, Inc.
300 Park Avenue South
New York, New York 10010
www.rizzoliusa.com

© 2004 by Ranjani Gopalarathinam
Design by Paul Kepple and Susan Van Horn at Headcase Design
www.headcasedesign.com
Cover illustration by Sujean Rim

2005 2006 2007 2008 2009 / 10 9 8 7 6 5 4 3 2 1
Distributed to the U.S. trade by Random House, New York
Printed in the United States of America
ISBN: 0-7893-1311-1
Library of Congress Catalog Control Number: 2005900425

Publisher's Note

Neither Universe nor the author has any interest, financial or personal, in the establishments listed in this book. No fees were paid or services rendered in exchange for inclusion in these pages. While every effort was made to ensure accuracy at the time of publication, it is always best to call ahead and confirm that the information is up-to-date.

contents

introduction

Shopping in New York City is not just a pastime; it is a way of life. For native New Yorkers, knowing the best places to shop for virtually anything (in a city where every imaginable thing is available) is a form of urban prowess. For visitors, New York is rife with people and activity the likes of which are unparalleled anywhere else, so even the smallest bit of information can be the chisel you need to start chipping away at the city's intimidating exterior. Whichever category you fall into, there is much to explore, and the city's mystery is part of what makes the hunt so tantalizing.

If you love to shop, New York will be the apex of your shopping life. If you are more interested in the cultural fabric of the city, shopping will give you an excuse, if not a great lens, on the kaleidoscope of neighborhoods, people, and hidden secrets that New York holds. Whatever your motivation, the city is always one step ahead of you and this guide will help you keep up with the brisk pace of New Yorkers while taking a tour of the city via its fabulous shops.

I have included veteran little shops, some exciting new spaces to check out in 2005, as well as numerous neighborhood R&R stops any day-tripper would enjoy. (Look to the sidebars for things to do while wandering through different neighborhoods.) Many of these shops are worth the visit alone whether you are buying or browsing, because part of the fun is in visiting their unique and varied showrooms. Other shops have a museum-like reverence for their wares (be it buttons or bathing suits) run by owners who carefully curate their selection of items so that you are seeing only the best and most representative items from upcoming lines, a service that spares you the hassle of wading through each season's fresh crop of new designers. The city is a puzzle of these little niches and viewpoints, and why New York shopping is world-famous.

While doing research for this book, I met some wonderful individuals in the different retail communities of the city, and I hope you will find the people you come across as fantastic as their little shops. I love New York, and the work I've done as a writer, producer, and trend forecaster has given me a great excuse to turn the city over and examine it from the inside out. There is so much to enjoy behind the grand facades of the buildings, around every corner, and even way up on the rooftops of the city, beyond what the naked eye can see.

how to use this book

This book is laid out by neighborhood, so wherever you begin your quest, take time to relax and enjoy the unique energy and spectacle of every New York City block you walk. There are also diversions you might chance upon while shopping—eating, drinking, pampering yourself—as well as useful services like tailors, cobblers, specific repair shops, and more. Gallery listings are woven throughout different downtown neighborhoods, since it's nice to pepper a shopping day with New York's unique artistic energy. You will find an alphabetical listing of stores in the back of the book as well as an index by shop type.

You'll tour the eclectic East Village, the finest home décor shops in the Meatpacking district, trendy Soho boutiques, and the pan-European flavor of the Upper East side. You may want to make a couple of jaunts to the up-and-coming neighborhoods in Brooklyn, including Williamsburg, where you will find a diverse range of stores nestled into vibrant communities. There are some better-known, larger shops mentioned in this book, but for the most part the focus is on small shops that reflect a true New Yorker's taste for the best in a city of infinite amusement and amazement. Enjoy!

east village

The East Village is a neighborhood that knows where it came from, where it's been, and where it's going. Once a part of the gritty Lower East Side, developers renamed the East Village in the 1980s to capture the cachet of historic Greenwich Village, and attract new residents. Today the neighborhood is one of the most eclectic and diverse in the city, and houses the oldest and youngest city residents side by side. For instance, old folks sit outside of their homes, playing cards, listening to music, and talking alongside hip new boutiques. Many brownstones have been recently renovated for NYU students and post-collegiate transplants, with state-of-the-art surveillance technology right next to community gardens such as the one on Avenue C (at E. 9th Street). As such the types of things you can find in the East Village range from centuries-old to cutting-edge. It's a great neighborhood to do some cool shopping and see how New Yorkers really live.

99X

❈ 84 East 10th Street bet. 3rd and 4th Avenues
HOURS: Mon–Sat 12–8, Sun 12–7
PHONE: 212-460-8599/8612
WEB: www.99xny.com

Where to stock a rocker's wardrobe—the birthplace of British punk style in New York City.

Lately, youth culture has been crying out for the grit of late '70s/early '80s NYC, and 99X has been around since before these babes were wailing. The store opened twenty-five years ago, and is in its third incarnation (its prior, exotic-sounding location, before 1991, was on East 6th Street "at the end of a crazy tunnel," says the store's manager). The owner's heritage is British, and she brought punk and ska-influenced brands, like Fred Perry, Doc Marten, Ben Sherman, and Lonsdale to the post–Vivienne Westwood and pre–Nirvana United States. 99X was the exclusive distributor of these now-popular brands for many years, before American fashion became hip to punk, and American department stores began retailing them. Amy Stevons, the store's buyer, says that the merchandise at 99X, which has always been "pretty much the same," has since come full circle to be coveted by a new generation. 99X could be considered the grandparent (or great-grandparent) of any rough-and-tumble teen rocker's look today.

You can find vestiges of a bygone punk era in the skinny suits hanging in the back of the store (up to $290), which the store custom makes for many local musicians. The store space is unobtrusive and far from pretentious. Upon closer examination, there is clearly a great deal of thought behind the buying. Most of the shoes, from classics like Vans to cutting-edge brands like Medium footwear, are limited-edition. Stevons says Vans and others create exclusives and higher-end lines for 99X not available to major retailers. The store also carries classic shoes like Creepers. Shoe prices range from $40–150, which is very reasonable for fashionable sneakers these days.

99X features the work of many fashion stylists and, over the years, has become a destination for the discerning punk connoisseur who, tragically, sports Fred Perry in the name of fashion, not ska.

scout

❊ 627 East 6th Street bet. Avenues B and C

HOURS: Daily 10:30–8:30

PHONE: 212-253-8987

WEB: www.scoutnyc.com

A one-stop shop for high-end and custom dog accessories, treats, clothing, furniture, and activities.

Scout boasts being the only upscale dog boutique in the down-to-earth East Village, and spares no detail in helping dog owners pamper their pets in style. Take the number of dogs who live in the East Village, add that to your average New Yorker's love of things high-end, and you have a claim to fame. Scout combines the best of fashion and fun for pet owners. Owner Karen Ngo discovered her dual passion for dogs and fashion in Tokyo, where she says pets are more integrated into their owners' lifestyles. "There are cafés in Tokyo where you can order food for you and your dog," she says.

The shop features doggie everything—stationery, toys ($4–20), furniture ($50–200), clothing ($25–150), specialty snacks ($1-12), bags ($75-300), and more. Karen is looking to expand the part of her store that sells custom doggie beds and other home interior items for dogs. People can pick fabrics for beds in any size then have them shipped anywhere. "In New York everyone is so eclectic with their taste, it's nice to be able to incorporate your dog's furniture into yours," she says.

Karen owns two dogs, and knows many of her clients from the popular dog run in Tompkins Square Park on East 10th Street. She utilizes the backyard and deck behind the store for community-building and social events for dog owners. In the past, she has thrown a '50s-style cabana pool party for Chihuahuas, replete with shabby-chic spread, Astroturf, and Martha Stewart–style doggie decorations. She throws a monthly "Leashes and Lovers" party, where singles with dogs can meet and socialize.

Karen also throws parties for dogs, and custom-orders dog-friendly cakes. Dogs eat special chicken-flavored cakes with no sugar, and no artificial ingredients or chemicals. Other human-grade treats at Scout include doggie sushi, doggie petit fours, pastries, Icelandic fish skins, Alaskan salmon treats, and salmon skin bones. (These dogs may be eating better than their human counterparts.)

In the future, she plans to offer a series of educational events, like crochet and knitting classes so people can learn to knit for their dogs, screen-printing T-shirts for both people and dogs, and a book club, where dog owners read dog-related books and share their perspectives with one another. She is keen on dog owners meeting each other. "Big dog owners care about food, while small dog owners are more into fashion for their dogs. We have a little something for all of them."

✓anna

�֍ 150 East 3rd Street bet. Avenues A and B
HOURS: Mon–Sat 1–8, Sun 1–7
PHONE: 212-358-0195
WEB: www.annanyc.com

Dance-inspired women's clothing that is versatile and sexy.

Kathy Kemp and her shop, Anna, pioneered the East Village girl's look in the late '90s, when the neighborhood was undergoing a radical transformation: sexy yet mobile. Today Anna thrives by selling dance-inspired, modern clothing, with a vintage influence. Kemp, who has designed for Mikhail

Baryshnikov's modern dance company, White Oak, makes clothing that expresses the shape and movement of a woman's body. For instance, a 1999 dress from Anna is a study in curves—a teal tube sheath with a lovely, sheer, stretchy overlaying dress piece that can be rouched and tied and scrunched. Anna's hot creations contain novel details while the overall shape flatters the body.

"I like to stay feminine and body conscious, but not be too trendy," Kathy explains. Kemp has basics in her store, making her a downtown Donna Karan. Standards are a tight-fitting trench coat "that fits *everyone*"; stripe faux wrap dresses that tie with ribbon sashes that "are sexy but not too sexy"; and now masculine/feminine shirts and suiting that complement a woman's curves. She designs pants with the idea that they can be worn with heels or rolled up and worn with flats to accommodate the day-to-night lifestyle so many young working women live in this city.

"Lots of things I do are things that can be worn a lot of different ways," she says. In fact, one 7-way top/dress, made of silk, comes with a booklet. Since Kathy does extremely limited production runs (she adds approximately three new items every week) she can use luxe fabrics from Italy, such as super-soft wool, ultra-soft cotton shirting, and silk.

Anna carries jewelry, like a sleek, natural wooden cuff from Cero Designs, and attractive pieces by Jenny Sheriff that are delicate, shiny works in metal. If all this doesn't sound like enough of a reason to hightail it down to the East Village, Kathy has a melting pot (literally, a basket) of vintage items, always $20 or less to mix and match with her designs. The clothes range from $50–250 (most are priced around or below $100); trench coats are $350; and the jewelry ranges from $85–150.

blue

❄ 137 Avenue A bet. St. Mark's Place and East 9th Street
HOURS: Mon–Fri 12–7, Sat–Sun 12–5, and by appointment
PHONE: 212-228-7744

Elegant but unconventional custom wedding and evening gowns by innovative, spunky veteran East Village designer.

The effortless style and charm of Greek-born designer Christina Kara is evident in her dresses, which are eye-catching even from out on the street. (In fact, several passersby stopped and gawked while she fitted a cream strapless dress with a tight box-pleat detail in the front on a mannequin.) She is definitely one of those people who fell into her profession naturally, having started out making cocktail dresses for friends, then eventually buying the shop ten years ago. Christina's dresses are certainly elegant, but they aren't conservative. "It's not that my dresses aren't balanced, but I want to capture the spirit of the moment," she says. Her dresses are elegant, but adventurous details—ruffles, hand-textured fabric, ribbons, unfinished edges—are what make them stunning. She also carries a breathtaking jewelry line by Eleni, made exclusively for Blue. The pieces are supposedly designed for brides, but if you like baubles, you won't wait until your wedding to pick them up. Eleni uses Mediterranean colors and stones like lapis blue and amethyst purple. One standout item was a beautiful multi-strand choker strung with three different sizes of alternating pearls. Jewelry ranges from $80–100; dresses start at $500 and go up to $4,000.

Exceptional Cleaners

These cleaners specialize in couture and bridal, and as such will do a great job with the jeans you refuse to put in the washing machine. They are on the expensive side, but are the best in the city.

Madame Paulette (1255 2nd Ave. bet. E. 65th and E. 66th Sts., Mon–Fri 7:30–7, Sat 8–5, 212-838-6827).

Chris French (57 4th Ave. at the corner of E. 9th St., Mon–Fri 7:30–7, Sat 8–5, 212-475-5444).

Have a Wedding Gift to Buy?

There are the shops where you know you can find something practical and sturdy; then there are other shops where possibilities you didn't know of exist. Why not make your shopping experience feel like less of a chore? Here are a couple of surefire and unusual places to find fabulous gifts for your bride- or groom-to-be friends, from high-end to style-end.

Tiffany's (5th Ave. at 57th St., Mon–Fri 10–7, Sat 10–6, Sun 12–5, 212-755-8000, Personal Shopping: 888-546-5188). I suppose no shopping guide would be complete without at least one mention of the classic jewelry made famous by Audrey Hepburn in 1961. It hasn't lost any of its charm—if anything, the designers at Tiffany's have infused the brand's classic, silver sensibility with fresh new ideas and trends. Tiffany gifts are still as timeless as the film.

At **Moss** (146 Greene St. bet. Houston and Prince Sts., Mon–Sat 11–7, Sun 12–6, 212-204-7100, www.mossonline.com) you can find housewares and gadgets that transform everyday experiences in the home into wondrous moments—objects float, shimmer, and inform the senses in ways that a traditional China set may not. Here you can find a conical cheese grater, a neon green wine rack, and a German-designed champagne whisk to de-bubble the bubbly that unfolds delicately like the foil from a piece of fine chocolate. See page 27 for more information.

And for a more international experience whether you're shopping for a bride or for some unique items to spice up your home décor…

Neera Saree Palace (131 Lexington Ave. bet. 28th and 29th Sts., Daily 11–7:30, 212-481-0325). Find bolts of sari fabrics, blouses, traditional outfits, jewelry, and more.

Butala Emporium (37–46 74th St. Jackson Heights, 718- 899-5590). Find traditional Indian candleholders in terra-cotta and silver, lanterns, incense holders, small idols, and other tchotchkes for use in ceremonies and centerpieces.

True Love Wedding Center (147 Bowery bet. Broome and Grand Sts., 212-625-1017). Traditional Chinese wedding dresses, photography, and invitations.

girly NYC

❊ 441 East 9th Street bet. Avenue A and 1st Avenue
HOURS: Wed–Mon 12–7, closed Tu
PHONE: 212-353-5366

Fun, glamorous, retro-influenced lingerie and nightwear by former T-shirt designer.

It's evident from the logo on the window of the store that Girly NYC isn't as straightforwardly precious as it sounds—there is something glamorous, retro, and definitely frisky in the curves of the type. Pam Atwood started designing lingerie after quirky T-shirt designs became commonplace. Her first line of underwear featured James Bond girls silk-screened onto sexy panties, and her sense of humor has only gotten more refined. Every girl who grew up in the '70s and '80s will appreciate the nod to the negligee in the fabrics and details (small rosebuds and bows) she uses, but the cuts and the styles, which recall Janet and Chrissy's getups on *Three's Company*, have been updated—cotton and lace tap shorts instead of terry cloth ones and an amazing nylon one-piece halter jumpsuit.

Pam has innovated much in the way of lingerie design, managing to combine fun, sexy, and comfortable into the package. Her lingerie separates are made mostly from nylon and cotton, but the colors and the lace trim are what make them special. She uses brights like orange, teal, violet, and dark periwinkle, as well as pastels like sea foam green and pink. Most of the panties are unconstructed bikinis and thongs cut low and straight across. The bras are cool too, very reminiscent of a first bra—triangle tops that are soft and comfortable in mesh fabric or the store's own nylon/spandex blend called "second skin." The cotton panties are especially cute, in the same bright colors, comfy cuts, and pretty lace trim. Her camisoles are striking contrasts in color, and one of the more popular camisoles has a cross-your-heart/rouching support structure. Another hot set was an entirely rouched bandeau bra top with matching boy shorts in fuschia. Nightwear includes nylon lounge pants with lace and rosebud details, and super soft cotton jersey negligees (in apple green with pink lace!).

Pam has been designing Girly for twelve years and selling it wholesale, but her East Village shop has only been around for a little over a year. Becoming part of the world of little shops has allowed Pam more room to experiment with fabrics and colors. The merchandise selection is expanding to include candles, jewelry, and other things that are fun, "but not too cute," she promises.

Panties start at $16, bras at $35, camisoles at $54, and some of the more specialty items (the jumpsuit, lace tap dancing shorts, etc.) start at $45 and up.

Sweet Nothings

Tired of the sterile, badly lit, messy, and generally unsavory lingerie sections at most department stores? Lucky for you some NYC retailers are revamping the environment and the merchandise. High-end, pretty lingerie is becoming the new shoe as far as sexy accessories go.

At **Henri Bendel** (712 5th Ave. bet. 55th and 56th Sts., Mon–Sat 10–7, Thu 10–8, Sun 12–6) look for a high-end lingerie department devoted entirely to young, hot new designers catering to younger women. Featured designers include Damaris, a British line whose signature cut involves knickers with a bow that ties in the back; Gentry de Paris, who makes lingerie out of cashmere jersey; and St. Tropez leisure, characterized by colorful two-tone lace panties.

Downtown, at discount giant **Century 21** (22 Cortlandt St., Mon–Fri 7:45–8, Sat 10–8, Sun 11–7, 212-227-9092) you can find beautiful stockings and lingerie (designers vary depending on what they get).

NY Stocking Exchange (189 Broadway bet. Cortlandt and Dey, Mon–Thu 8–7, Fri 8–7:30, Sat 11–6, closed Sun, 212-233-4116) looks like a Frederick's of Hollywood but actually stocks reputable lingerie brands like the extremely popular Cosabella.

At **Azaleas** (223 E. 10th St. bet. 1st and 2nd Aves. Tu–Fri 1–8, Sat 12–8, Sun 1–6, closed Mon, 212-253-

5484, www.azaleasnyc.com) you can find a super selection of reasonably priced bras, panties, garters, slips, swimwear, dresses, and more. Azaleas carries more than thirty lingerie designers (see the web site for a complete listing) including Belabumbum, La Cosa, On Gossamer, Woo, and Hanky Panky.

Only Hearts (230 Mott St. bet. Prince and Spring Sts., Mon–Sat 11–7, Sun 12–6, 212-431-3694). Only Hearts designer Helena Stewart originated the mesh lingerie craze (knocked off by brands like On Gossamer and Cosabella). You can buy boy shorts and bikinis in Delicious (a nylon/Lycra blend) or mesh, trimmed in lace, for $18–40. The standard colors are white, birch, and black, in addition to any seasonal colors. The bras are cool too, very reminiscent of a first bra—triangle tops that are soft and comfortable, in mesh or second skin. The shop also sells velvet blazers and coats, ultra-feminine skirts, and pliable crewneck mesh shirts in rich jewel tones like burgundy, ruby, and turquoise. The tops sell for under $100, and the pants and jackets start at $200 and up. (Also uptown at 386 Columbus Ave. bet. W. 78th and W. 79th Sts., Mon–Sat 11–8, Sun 11–6, 212-724-5608).

Mixona (262 Mott St. bet. E. Houston and Prince Sts., Daily 11–7:30, 646-613-0100) features ultra-sexy dressing rooms draped in crimson red silk that are spacious enough to accommodate a guest while you are trying on the crème de la crème of saucy lingerie by La Perla, Christian Stott, Ravage, La Cosa, and more.

Down in Soho—and when I say down, I mean way down—**Agent Provocateur** (133 Mercer St. bet. Prince and Spring Sts., Mon–Sat 11–7, Sun 12–6, 212-965-0229) makes the wickedest, most beautiful lingerie you've ever seen in their bordello of a boutique. The designers, John Corre (Vivienne Westwood's son) and his wife Serena

Rees, have designed different lines of lingerie for different occasions—from flirty to downright naughty (whips cost $225). The most popular all-around (read: recreational or otherwise) item is the AP corset, which comes in all black or a very pale pink with black ribbon detail and is sold out on the web site ($216). The panties and bras are exquisitely crafted and have pin-up girl names. Most bras cost around $100. If you are in the market for super flattering, luxurious undergarments and have some cash to spend, there's no store in the city that will make you feel (or look) hotter than Agent Provocateur.

Toys in Babeland (43 Mercer St., bet. Broome and Grand Sts., Mon–Sat 12–9, Sun 12–7, 212-966-2120). This shop runs the gamut, from sex toys to empowerment! The owners, Claire Cavanah and Rachel Venning, opened the store to create an environment that promotes and celebrates sexual vitality in all women. Inspired by the lack of "normal" sex toy shops in Seattle, they opened their first shop in 1993 and now have two New York locations. The shops attempt to create a positive environment, and their pro-woman, pro-sex outlook has been infectious for women of all ages, as well as couples. Toys you will find at the shop are colorful and interesting and are accompanied by descriptions and helpful information about each. Toys in Babeland offers seminars, and you can browse books and talk to the staff without feeling weird about it. Look at their web site for more information about the company, the merchandise (they do mail-order), and a blog. The owners also authored a book called *Sex Toys 101* in 2003 that details practically every toy available on the market. (Also on the Lower East Side at 94 Rivington St. bet. Ludlow and Orchard Sts., Mon–Sat 12–10, Sun 12–7, 212-375-1701).

While you're in the East Village...

Check out the **Russian and Turkish Baths** on E. 10th St. bet. 1st and 2nd Aves., 212-473-8806) which opened in 1892. Wow! Take a walk on the old (and steamy) side, by visiting this East Village institution. For a mere $25, you can spend the day at these aged and surprisingly well-preserved bathhouses. Towels and locks are provided, and there are women-only and men-only mornings during the week (the rest of the times are coed).

The entire lower level of the building is the bath, with enclosures for Russian and Swedish sauna rooms (the difference is steam versus heat, respectively). There is a cold dunking pool for a refresher, as well as a sun deck upstairs once you are all steam-cleaned. The Russian Baths are an Old World-style experience where men and women of all ages come together to do...nothing! In New York City, that is a beautiful thing.

Once you've cleansed your skin, your mind, and your worries away, you can go across the street to **Live Live** (261 E. 10th St. bet. 1st and 2nd Aves., 212-505-5504), a shop that sells locally made raw snacks and munchies, potions, lotions and oils, raw food cookbooks (recommended), and other literature about the raw food movement.

If you want to make it a total daylong experience, you can end by having dinner nearby at **Quintessence** (263 E. 10th St., 646-654-1804) a gourmet raw food restaurant that features entrees and desserts made of entirely raw ingredients. I highly recommend the dessert-as-meal route at Quintessence—you'd be surprised how filling the food is.

✓ 3 turtle doves

�֟ 201 E. 2nd St. bet. Avenues A and B
HOURS: Tu–Sun 1–10, closed Mon
PHONE: 212-529-3288

*A charming new and vintage accessories saloon
with a feminine, playful, and western vibe.*

3 Turtle Doves is a spaghetti Western movie set for girls, replete with wooden beams and low lighting. The space is a dressing room-saloon with vintage and new accessories of an Americana bent hanging on pegs and branches around the store. Heather Ramie and her partner are self-described "girly" girls. They feed their appetite for fantasy and imagination with their merchandise. What stands out is the jewelry, which is unusual and beautifully crafted. Highlights are Hannah Clark's naturalistic designs, as well as Bella New York's gold filigree disks, a welcome alternative to the chandelier earring. Ivana makes contrasting crocheted ponchos and handbags. From Kathleen Dreska come wedding/engagement bands (by appointment only). Regina Early provides costume-influenced headpieces as well as baby moccasins. Jewelry ranges from $45–375, depending on the material. Bags by Lilith NYC stand out as the best new handbags in the store, slouchy suede totes with leather details in dusty floral hues ($150). The store also features handmade dog clothing (from $35–150), vintage Izod, cameras, and more.

The two women partner with other East Village businesses to produce one-off (special pieces made for one occasion, sometimes a sample or a custom order) items for promotional use and parties, such as custom-made dog hats for a party at **Scout** (See pg. 8).

amarcord

❊ 84 E. 7th St. bet. 1st and 2nd Avenues

HOURS: Wed–Sat 12–8, closed Sun, Mon, Tu

PHONE: 212-614-7133

WEB: www.amarcordvintagefashion.com

Pristine Italian vintage clothing and accessories for high fashion lovers.

The luxury, glamour and style of Italian New Wave films are alive and well at this bastion of European vintage clothing and accessories. Named eponymously for the quintessential Fellini film featuring super glam and gorgeous movie stars, Amarcord's owners passionately believe in the die-hard connection between fashion and the immortality of the moving image. Owners Marco Liotta and Patti Bordoni are both vintage veterans, having spent years at the flea markets in Chelsea. Bordoni grew up in fashion in Italy, where his grandfather was a tailor. The clothing, shoes, and handbags at Amarcord are nothing short of exquisite. Everything is color-coded and in phenomenal condition: Sophia Loren–style Italian knits, trench coats, skirts, and dresses hang impeccably like pristine historical relics. Amarcord carries new designers, such as the Italian accessories designer Roberta di Camarino and Sergio Rossi (118 Wooster St. bet. Prince and Spring Sts., Mon–Sat 10–7, Sun 12–6, 212-941-0529). Their vintage selection includes rare Gucci bags, Dior, YSL, Celine, and Missoni. Taking a cue from Fellini, there's great humor in Liotta and Bordoni's accessories choices: yellow patent leather and Lucite details, flat metallic and gold accents.

Prices vary widely depending on the item—the average cost of shoes is $150, handbags average around $200, and clothing starts at $30, depending on the item.

Besides another retail location in Williamsburg (at 223 Bedford Ave. bet. N. 4th and N. 5th Sts., Daily 1–8, 718-963-

4001) which carries similarly fabulous but slightly more eclectic merchandise, the couple owns a Phantom Tollbooth–like warehouse that transports visitors back to a time when men and women worth their salt were unbelievably glamorous. Located near the Williamsburg shop, the storage facility houses 16,000 pieces, which are not for sale, but available only for viewing by appointment. Call the Williamsburg location for details.

john derian co.

☀ 6 East 2nd Street bet. Bowery and 2nd Avenue
HOURS: Tu–Sun 12–7, closed Mon
PHONE: 212-677-3917
WEB: www.johnderian.com

Organic crafting meets modern design in this East Village home and lifestyle boutique.

Walking through John Derian's shop is like taking a stroll through a foliage-covered backyard path that winds and twists past exquisite birdbaths and other beautiful decorative objects. Derian has been doing *decoupage*—cut paper on glass—for over fourteen years, and carries his line of dishes and housewares in the store (dishes range from $14–500). His new line, as well as more information about the art of decoupage, can be found on his web site. Other merchandise is nineteenth century European inspired, but there is a lively and organic feeling of color, texture, and nature in the space as well. The store carries smaller French and American furniture lines, with antiques interspersed throughout. Textiles folded and draped all over the store emphasize the idea of being cozy at home. Featured textile designers include Lisa Corti, who uses hand-block printed textiles from India in her collection, and Elsa C., who makes home textiles that marry

Age of Enlightenment prints with modern cotton fabrics. Quilts range from $240–1200 in price, while pillows are $55–200. Moroccan lanterns and leather poufs ($200) throw a pinch of spice into the mix. Amidst the many handmade knickknacks, Derian has featured the artwork of British artist Hugo Guinness, who makes original collages and woodblock prints on paper ($350–1100). I was intrigued by local artist Alex Carlton's T-shirts and sweatshirts, which were the perfect blend of lived-in and hip, via heavy metal and nature-inspired imagery of the '80s ($55–110).

In the future, Derian says we can look forward to another downtown location. Wholesale customers can buy both his and imported designs online (the T-shirts, I should note, are not for sale on the site).

la reina

✣ 100 Avenue C bet. East 6th and 7th Streets
HOURS: Tu–Sun 1–8, closed Mon
PHONE: 212-475-3889

Costume-worthy vintage from every decade fills this Alphabet City boutique, with fabulous accessories for every mood and trend.

Los Angeles native Leanna Zuniga is completely at ease in the beautiful environs of La Reina. Vintage is more accessible and popular in L.A., and Zuniga tries to convey that quality in her comprehensive Alphabet City shop. La Reina specializes in mint-condition pieces made from the highest-quality fabrics: silks, wools, and more—no polyester here! The store stocks vintage from various decades, but the highlights are in items that could have come from the sets of *The King and I* or *The Ten Commandments*—gold, white, elaborately beaded and brocade details pop out from everywhere. Attractively merchandised, every item stands completely on its own—a blue silk dress from the 1940s hangs right next to an impeccable pair of off-white tuxedo trousers from the 1970s.

La Reina is known for its accessories, which fashion stylists often rent and borrow from Zuniga for fashion shoots. The accessories are simple '80s plastic to vintage art deco at different price ranges. She has accessories to go with every current look—beads, brooches, plastic, and more.

Zuniga says she likes to keep the store "pure," meaning she only stocks vintage. She buys her vintage from all over the world—London, Germany, Miami, and Los Angeles. She cites Yves Saint Laurent as one of her favorite designers. Having grown up "surrounded by mountains of fabric" (her grandmother was a seamstress who was known as "la reina" or "queen" in Spanish) so Zuniga knows quality vintage. Her main price point is $65, which is reasonable considering the exclusive beauty and detail in each piece. This store is a treasure chest waiting to be opened by those smart enough to uncover it.

compact impact

✳ 21 Avenue B bet. East 2nd and 3rd Streets
HOURS: Tu–Sat 11–10, Sun 11–7, closed Mon
PHONE: 212-677-0500
WEB: www.compactimpact.com

Compact Impact carries a mostly Japanese inventory of small products and gadgets for work and home that are innovative in design and functionality.

The shop space is a spare concrete and wood science fiction-style hideout where ideas are bubbling. Most items are simple, inexpensive, and easy to use—a primer in how technology will influence our lifestyles in years to come. Along the walls, gadgets are showcased for demonstration. Far from pretentious or complicated, most of the products are the result of simple ideas executed at a micro-level. Some standout items are DIY cardboard speakers from Muji ($35); magnetic jewelry ($50–100); portable power sources and USB connections (under $20); and hi-tech food and drink. There are toys by Takashi Murakami at $20 a pop, affordable art for the masses. Sneakers by Sou Sou are modern takes on the traditional Japanese tabi shoe (the kind where the big toe is separate from the rest of the foot) and printed like Vans.

Compact Impact sponsors monthly evening events, called Compact Impact Nights, where artists, scientists, and technologists can get together and discuss developments in the area of interactive art, technology, and the future. The store is open late, making it a great spot to get your technology fix after grabbing dinner or a drink.

The store's web site is comprehensive in its catalog of future-reaching products for the home. There are more products available on the web site than in the store, which is apparently where the truly forward shop.

Photos Fast

You're in town for a short time, you had a great day checking out the city, and you want to show some friends the photos at a dinner they have planned for you tomorrow night. Here are some places that are open late, do it quick, and don't charge an arm and a leg.

Manhattan Color Labs (4 W. 20th St. at 5th Ave., Mon–Fri 7–midnight, Sat–Sun 9–6, 212-807-7373). The technicians here are skilled, reasonable, and nice. For $12 they do a killer job on 36 4 x 6-inch color prints.

At **Soho Photolab** (395 Canal St. bet. Thompson St. and W. Broadway, Mon–Fri 9:30–7, Sat 11–5, 212-274-0365) they can turn around beautiful prints in as little as 30 minutes ($17).

C-Lab (650 Broadway near Bleecker St., Mon–Fri 8–11, Sat–Sun 9–5, 212-228-2522) specializes in printing color film. They are open late and do the best specialty jobs (that is, if you want 4 x 5 prints, enlargements, or anything out of the ordinary).

soho

From specialty boutiques to flagships, Soho is the mecca for shopping in New York City. It is one of the most awe-inspiring and historical neighborhoods in the city, but it also houses the most retail per block. Once filled with fabric warehouses, printing houses, and artists' lofts, Soho has become one of the most heavily trafficked neighborhoods downtown, especially on weekends. New Yorkers lament its transformation but don't miss out on the fantastic shopping Soho has to offer. The scene is still colorful and lively, from street vendors and artists to pedestrians walking by.

Most major brands have stores in Soho now, and last year **Bloomingdale's** opened a downtown location to cater to a younger customer (504 Broadway bet. Prince and Spring Sts., Mon–Fri 10–9, Sat 10–8, Sun 11–7). The **Apple** computer store (103 Prince St. at Greene St., Mon–Sat 10–8, Sun 11–7, 212-226-3126), is always brimming with people playing with gadgets, visiting one of the seminars upstairs, or just people watching. If you aren't a Mac user, you may become one after checking out the amply spaced displays of computers, peripherals, and electronics.

Stores which have outposts here in addition to midtown Fifth Avenue flagships include: Louis Vuitton, Burberry, Prada, Miu Miu, Emporio Armani, Joseph, Max Mara, Michael Kors, DKNY, Polo by Ralph Lauren, and many more. Most of these stores line the five to six blocks going west from Broadway to Sixth Avenue, along Prince and Spring streets. There's plenty to do in Soho. You could easily kill four or five hours browsing, shopping, and watching the beautiful people walk by.

moss

✼ 146 Greene Street bet. Houston and Prince Streets
HOURS: Mon–Sat 10–7, Sun 12–6.
PHONE: 212-204-7100
WEB: www.mossonline.com

Industrial design mecca that caters to aficionados and curious passersby with a sumptuous collection of housewares, furniture, appliances, books, and more.

Moss is a virtual museum of contemporary industrial design, having started as a gallery in Soho in 1994. Merchandise ranges from the practical—a pocket knife, a clock radio—to the outrageous, such as an oblong blue and silver tweed lip-shaped sofa retailing for $13,000. Interesting objects abound and the staff is knowledgeable and friendly. If the sofa isn't in your budget, check out the books at the southern end of the store—they have a terrific selection of artist monographs and other design/architecture tomes, including works by Bruce Mau, Jasper Morrison, and more. In late 2004, Moss expanded its reach into the ground floor of the luxury condominium building on the corner of Greene and East Houston Street for art shows and other in-store events.

Galleries in Soho

Whether you're in the market for a great piece of art or not, it's great to add a dash of culture to your shopping experience in Soho. A short list of a few great Soho galleries:

The Drawing Center (35 Wooster St. bet. Grand and Broome Sts., Tu–Fri 10–6, Sat 11–6, closed Mon and Sun, 212-219-2166), and **Spencer Brownstone Gallery** (39

Wooster St. bet. Grand and Broome Sts., Tu–Sat 10:30–6, closed Sun and Mon, 212-334-3455), side by side, are two of the best. They feature up-and-coming artists who specialize in politically charged illustrations and drawings.

The Visionaire Gallery (11 Mercer St. bet. Grand and Canal Sts., Mon–Fri 9–6, Sat 1–6, closed Sun, 212-274-8959) is home to the notoriously decadent fashion magazine *V* and collector's edition Visionaire books. They mostly show photography and designer objects.

Avant garde art dealer Jeffery Deitch shows a wide variety of artworks at the smaller of his two galleries, **Deitch Projects** (76 Grand St. bet. Greene and Wooster Sts., hours vary depending on the show, 212-343-7300). Deitch's roster is varied, featuring artists like the electronic music and dance performance troupe Fischerspooner. The gallery's shows often reflect the current trend in artwork that references entertainment, technology, and pop culture.

untitled

❈ 159 Prince St. bet. Thompson Street and West Broadway
HOURS: Sun–Thu 10–8, Fri–Sat 10–9
PHONE: 212-982-2088
WEB: www.fineartinprint.com

Soho stationer and art bookstore featuring handmade cards and eccentric postcards from every era.

You don't find many small, quiet shops like Untitled in Soho anymore, mainly because of the explosion of commercial retailers through its cobbled streets in the last ten years. Fortunately, the store's expertise and old-world feel thrives in this changing neighborhood. Untitled sits on the fence between the past and the present, housing hundreds of absurd and obscure postcards, handmade stationery, greeting cards, and various paper gift items. The postcards are organized by categories like "Beach Ball, 1930" and "Absurd, 1920." The books shoot us back to the present. Untitled provides an expert, up-to-the-minute selection of graphic design, typography, art, and architecture criticism from all over the world. You can find books about Duchamp alongside works of newer contemporary artists. A more spacious branch of the store on West Broadway features an extensive art book collection, but it lacks the spontaneous, eccentric feel of the original.

Untitled is easily the best place in the city to buy a greeting card that is guaranteed to please. Many of the cards are handmade with intimate messages well worth the $5–15 they cost; others are slightly simpler in design ($2.50 and up) but are always different, smart, and witty, sporting great pop culture references and photos. If sentimental greeting cards rub you the wrong way, you will find a great alternative at Untitled.

Paper Shops

Great paper can make a bold statement, as many busy New Yorkers will testify. Whether you are buying a gift, putting together a job application, or dropping someone an enticing note, here is an assortment of some paper shops around the city where you are likely to find high quality, unique stationery, notebooks, and pens.

JAM Paper and Envelope (135 3rd Ave. bet. E. 14th and E. 15th Sts., Mon–Fri 8:30–7, Sat–Sun 10–6, 212-473-6666, www.jampaper.com) has locations from the east to west side downtown because they stock paper in the brightly colored hues more traditional stationery stores shy away from. They also print business cards cheaply on bright (or not) colored card stock. (Also at 611 6th Ave. at W. 18th St., 212-255-4593.)

Kate's Paperie (561 Broadway bet. Prince and Spring Sts., Mon–Sat 10–8, Sun 11–7, 212-941-9816, www.katespaperie.com). This is probably the most popular place in the city—both by reputation and location—to find stationery and other paper products, including fancy gift wrap, ribbon, bags and boxes, planners, invitations, photo frames, albums, and all kinds of other containing, framing, organizing, and fun stuff. Kate's carries indulgent bonds and stocks, as well as luxury items for the study, credenzas, and fancy letter openers and the like. They stock a terrific selection of pens as well. Check the web site for an online store.

Pearl Paint (308 Canal St. bet. Broadway and Mercer St., Mon–Fri 9–7, Sat 10–6:30, Sun 10–6, 212-431-7932, www.pearlpaint.com) is the mother of all art stores in the city, and you can find virtually any framing, storage, or archiving material here, as well as a range of papers, paints, pens, albums, tools, and more. The store is five floors of anything you could possibly need to fulfill any creative urge and prices are reasonable. Check their web site for details.

Paper Presentation (23 W. 18th St. bet. 5th and 6th Aves., Mon 9–7, Tu–Thu 9–8, Fri 9–7, Sat 11–6, Sun 12–6, 212-463-7035). This spacious store, just north of Union Square, stocks materials for archiving letters and photos, stationery, picture frames, and unusual greeting cards.

Cat Fish Greetings Inc. (219A Mulberry St. bet. Spring and Broome Sts., Mon–Sat 10:30–8, Sun 12–6, 212-625-1800) specializes in greeting card and invitation designs created with special textured paper. The store has a catalog of the simple, contemporary designs it offers. If you have a sense of humor about special occasions, this is a great place to find some stationery or a greeting card. The combination of ink-on-paper with a three dimensional blending of fine papers and objects make the cards tactile and fun. Cat Fish also sells great Japanese and technology-inspired gifts like desk accessories, CD cases, albums, and more. Prices for stationery run from $10 and up; greeting cards are $5.

You Got the Write Stuff, Baby

Some people love cars. Others, shoes. And some of us, pens. Going to write something? Gotta have a great pen. Here are three renowned pen stores in Manhattan, in order from oldest to youngest, where you will find the pen of your dreams.

Fountain Pen Hospital (10 Warren St. bet. Broadway and Church St. in Tribeca, Mon–Fri 7:45–5:45, Sat–Sun 9–5:30, 212-964-0580). The store was founded in 1946, and this family business continues to be the granddaddy of writing implements in the city. Did you know there was a magazine called *Pen World* or *The Pennant*? Me neither, but if you know someone who loves pens, they might be delighted to hear that the owner is a regular contributor to these publications. Seriously, find any pen your heart desires here. Special and custom orders available—just visit the store.

Joon (Grand Central Terminal, Lexington Ave. at 42nd St., Mon–Fri 8–8, Sat 10–6, Sun 12–5, 212-949-1702) is another New York pen institution. They carry your Parker, your Mont Blanc, your Fisher, your

Cartier...need I say more? Located inside Grand Central, this is a good excuse for you to visit one of the most beautiful buildings in New York and then write to your mom about it. (Also at 782 Lexington Ave. at 61st St., 212-935-1007; Lobby Level, Trump Tower, 725 5th Ave. at 57th St., 212-317-8466; and 3 World Financial Center, 200 Vesey St. at the Winter Garden Atrium, 212-227-0557.)

Berliner Pen (928 Broadway, Suite 203, Mon–Fri 10–1, 212-614-3020). Berliner Pen sells both vintage and contemporary writing instruments. They also provide services such as repairing older, hard-to-service pens, and museum quality restoration services to antique pens. It's heartening to think about pens being preserved as the artifacts they are quickly becoming.

eye candy

❋ 329 Lafayette Street bet. Bleecker and Houston Streets
HOURS: Mon–Sat 12–8, Sun 12–6
PHONE: 212-343-4275
WEB: www.eyecandystore.com

A dazzling array of vintage, estate, and new costume jewelry and accessories, including handbags and sunglasses.

The day I visited Eye Candy, I trailed Gwen Stefani of the band No Doubt up Broadway, where she was shopping with her entourage. Ms. Stefani completely exemplifies how a classic look and modern style clash to perfection and would probably love the glittery goodness of Eye Candy, a comprehensive new and vintage jewelry shop. At the time the store opened six years ago, there were not as many accessories-only stores. Eye

Candy still stands out as a destination for the jewelry fanatic.

"It's yin and yang with vintage and fashion. All the designers are in here because vintage looks inspire them six months before we see their lines," owner Ron Caldwell says. He buys vintage jewelry that has a modern feel, and can be mixed with everyday clothes. Fittingly, Perry Ellis embellished its runway looks for fall 2004 with brooches from Eye Candy. The pieces in the store are unusual, bright, and colorful, if not downright fabulous. If you are looking for a little sass and flash this is a great place to visit. What is fun about the shop is that the new pieces are mixed with the vintage ones, so you never know what you are getting into until you check out the price tag. In this sense, Eye Candy definitely brings the modern shopper up to speed in vintage accessories.

The shop sells handbags and sunglasses as well as jewelry. Vintage jewelry ranges from $50–300, new pieces are $20–150, and other accessories are $40–300.

Baubles To Party In!

Sometimes, you are looking for something simple to spice up a dress or a sweater or a skirt. You want fun but sophisticated jewelry without a high-end price tag. With the resurgence in popularity of costume jewelry, there are some party jewelry manufacturers who tastefully knock off vintage styles from the 1970s and 80s.

Girlprops.com (153 Prince St. at W. Broadway, Sun–Thu 10–9, Fri–Sat 10–10, 212-505-7615. Also in the East Village at 33 E. 8th St. bet. University Place and Broadway). Judging from the outside of Girlprops.com, you would never think that you could find something that was passable for a woman over fifteen—the awning is striped in a zebra pattern and the lettering looks like something straight out of *Tiger Beat* magazine. Don't let the initial glare of glitter deceive you—all along the walls and inside the hundreds of bins at this small downstairs boutique, you will find all kinds of well-made, low-cost costume hair accessories, earrings, necklaces, and more. Granted, if you have a teen in your life, she would love it here, too. However, who said that you have to be eleven to appreciate hair barrettes and clips shaped like jeweled butterflies and other mythical creatures, beads of all shapes and sizes, and brooches galore?

Marc by Marc Jacobs (403 Bleecker St. at W. 11th St., Mon–Sat 11–7, Sun 12–6, 212-924-0026). You might be wondering what Marc Jacobs is doing underneath the "Queen of Costume Jewelry" shop. The reason is that his shop in the Meatpacking District has great gumball machines that dispense accessories in the front of the store. You don't have to go into the shop to get to them. Inside the clear bubbles are brooches, rings, and necklaces that are ready to wear. So, you might have spent $3000 on a suit, but who needs to know that you only spent fifty cents on the brooch?

zakka

❄ 147 Grand Street bet. Crosby and Lafayette Streets
HOURS: Wed–Mon 12–7, closed Tu
PHONE: 212-431-3961
WEB: www.zakkacorp.com

A bookstore specializing in graphic design and art books, with a special emphasis on Asian pop culture, toys, and graffiti.

This Japanese-owned bookstore calls itself a "shop and space for creators." Japanese artists have pioneered some subcultures in art and music, and Zakka compiles and cross-references these movements to perfection. The shop's mainstay is graphic arts-related books, as well as new and old titles on contemporary art, architecture, illustration, and design. The bookstore is geared toward graphic designers, animators, illustrators, and other artists working in a commercial capacity, and the books examine the construction of images and ideas we see every day. Books sell from $20–100.

Additionally, upcoming artists like Kaws and others exhibit their work through for-sale products like T-shirts, toys, and other collectibles. Zakka's in-house team designs innovative T-shirt graphics (around $30). My particular favorites are the UGLY dolls, which were designed to be an antidote to the typical, precious image of a doll or soft toy. Each doll is a soft, quirky character with its own story, and their bizarre, squeezable bodies fit snugly under your arm. They cost $19 (most of the toys are in this price range), making them great gifts for anyone tall or small. The web site is fun to browse, and very comprehensive. If you'd like to research a particular book or other item before visiting the shop, check it out.

Other Awesome Bookstores

New York is known for its culture and politics, and much of the starting places for all kinds of debates are in bookstores. These bookstores are great alternatives to the major chains.

St. Mark's Bookshop in the East Village (31 3rd Ave. at E. 9th St., Daily 10–midnight, 212-260-7853) is legendary for its selection of subversive and thought-provoking books.

At the **Tokion bookshop** (78 Clinton St. bet.

Delancey and Rivington Sts. in the Lower East Side, 212-358-9818), explore the movement of a new class of creative professionals and artists, like graphic designers, illustrators, and fashion designers, at the forefront of contemporary art.

The New Museum bookstore (556 W. 22nd St. bet. 9th and 10th Aves., Tu, Wed, Fri 12–6, Thu 12–8, closed Sun and Mon, 212-343-0460) is unparalleled in its selection of books about art, books that are art, and everything in between.

The Housing Works Bookstore and Café (126 Crosby St. bet. Prince and Houston Sts., Mon–Fri 10–9, Sat 12–9, Sun 12–7, 212-334-3324) is a great place to go pick up that Russian novel you never finished in college and read it leisurely, overlooking picturesque cobbled Crosby Street. No one will bother you, no one will come collect what you're reading, and you can stay from morning until night.

At **Clovis Books** in Williamsburg (229 Bedford Ave. bet. N. 4th and N. 5th Sts., Mon–Sun 11–10, 718-302-3751), you can find a mix of beautiful secondhand hardcover fiction, art books, and little art press zines and limited edition literature and art books.

At **Unoppresive, Non-Imperialist Bargain Books** (34 Carmine St. bet. Bedford and Bleecker Sts., Mon–Thu 11–10, Fri 11–11, Sat 12–11, Sun 12–8, 212-229-0078) in Greenwich Village, find dirt cheap editions of classics, from the *Bhagavad Gita* to *Catcher in the Rye* to graphic novels. $3 and up for new books.

Uptown at **Ursus Books and Prints, Limited** (981 Madison Ave. bet. E. 76th and E. 77th Sts., Mon–Fri 10–6, Sat 11–5, closed Sun, 212-772-8787), you can find rare, out-of-print, and new art reference books.

opening ceremony

❄ 35 Howard Street bet. Crosby and Lafayette Streets
HOURS: Mon–Sat 11–8, Sun 12–7
PHONE: 212-219-2688
WEB: www.openingceremony.com

Edgy downtown store with an international roster of fashion and accessory designers.

Competition for most things is fierce in this city, and the owners of Opening Ceremony took up the challenge of presenting their customers with something different. Each season, Humberto Leon and Carol Lim feature a range of international design talents who "compete" against a team of U.S. designers, headed by their own label, Opening Ceremony.

The store concept originated from a shopping trip to Hong Kong, where many vendors sell disparate items out of separate spaces—Humberto and Carol wanted to pull these items together under one roof. The duo was inspired by Baron Pierre de Coubertin, who experienced the defining moment of his life when he founded the Olympics. The result is a selection of merchandise from a rotating cast of international designers, keeping the store's vibe fresh and interesting.

The standing New York design team includes Benjamin Cho, Indigo People, Cloak, Mary Ping and Slow and Steady Wins the Race, Rachel Comey, Saved (look for the **Saved Gallery**, p. 118), the signature Opening Ceremony collection, and more. Their line is clean, innovative, and simple—the basics with a twist—fleece blazers, oversized hoodies, and embellished woven shirts. Rachel Comey makes novel, feminine tops by experimenting with shapes and patterned fabrics. Indigo People makes a subtle and nuanced collection of office and street wear and experiments with color. All of the lines demonstrate a commitment to innovation either in fabric or design. Prices range from $25–395 for clothing,

$200–1200 for coats, and $10–295 for shoes and accessories.

"The more popular labels are always the visiting country collections, because they are all new and fresh and only sold in our store," Humberto says. "The U.S. collections do well, too, because we buy the collections the way we would buy clothes for our closet!" The two owners handpick everything, and as such, "everything is our favorite." You can find the best of the familiar, the strange, and the exclusive under one roof. One-of-a-kind vintage and select items from the country's open-air markets are also included.

In 2005, the duo will feature a German shop on the second level of the immense store that will be curated by the German design team, Bless. Some German lines to look for are Vera & Daphne Correll, Schiesser Revival, Wolfen, Frank Leder, Adidas, Pulver, and Fluo. The store still carries designers who have been featured in the past, such as Brazilian Alexander Herchcovitch, who has designed Hello Kitty T-shirts for Japanese toy giant Sanrio.

nom de guerre

❊ 640 Broadway, underground gate entrance at the
southeast corner of Broadway and Bleecker Street
HOURS: Mon–Sat 12–8, Sun 12–7
PHONE: 212-253-2891

Urban-tinged high fashion meets limited-edition footwear and artist-designed clothing in an underground gallery space.

There aren't many shops like Nom de Guerre, where fashion meets art and street culture in such perfect synchronicity. It is modeled after an Army-Navy store, and inhabits the former meeting space of the Black Panthers. The clothing is sleek basics with subversive details and high-quality finishing. The four owners have diverse backgrounds in fashion design, media, and art. They have created a unique multi-label store that utilizes artwork, music, and design to cater to a particularly fashion-forward urban shopper. The store is kept almost intentionally covert—on the street outside the shop is a sandwich board that says "Copy Shoppe Downstairs," with an arrow pointing down, into the clubhouse.

The in-house label Nom de Guerre features simple redesigns of classic street wear for both men and women. Throughout the collection, utilitarian ideals meet fine finishing, so you end up with a jacket, a hoodie, or a shirt that can easily be worn under a suit or with a pair of jeans. There are artist-issued T-shirts by Devon Ojas and others that use metallic inks, bold colors, and burners (elaborate graffiti pieces) as the basis for their design. Denim and outerwear designers include A.P.C. and Earnest Sewn, a denim line designed by the makers of Paper Denim and Cloth. Both use minimal elements to create basic pieces that are über-stylish and functional.

Other designers are more fashion-oriented, including Tess Giberson and As Four, who have both enjoyed recent commercial success with their innovative lines. The store also carries Nike limited-edition sneakers that you would be hard pressed to find anywhere else in the city. If you are serious about shopping New York City–style, at Nom de Guerre you have it in the palm of your hand—loose, practical, and stylish.

The owners maintain a popular Williamsburg clothing store called **Isa** (88 N. 6th St., Mon–Fri 1–9, Sat 12–10, Sun 12–8, 718-387-3363), which houses some of the same designers, and more local designers, in a 2,000-square-foot retail space.

Blue Jeans

In Soho and Nolita, fashion rules. Billboards and models abound. Fortunately, for the rest of us, fashion has embraced the everyday luxury of denim, and there is a symphony of denim washes, styles, and looks on the market. In New York, people take their denim very seriously. As such, there are a few boutiques reflecting the different shades of the spectrum.

At **Built By Wendy** (7 Centre Market Place bet. Broome and Grand Sts., Mon–Sat 12–7, Sun 12–6, 212-925-6538), you can find great American/country-influenced shirting and a new line of Wrangler jeans for men and women by the designer (from $150). These are classic blues, cut a bit higher in the waist and straighter in the leg, perfect for tucking into your cowboy boots.

At **Selvedge** in Nolita (150 Mulberry St. bet. Prince and Spring Sts., Mon–Sat 11–7, Sun 12–6, 212-219-0994), you can find vintage and hard-to-find styles of Levi's, whether you are a style-conscious urban cowgirl or a real cowboy. The store resembles a tack room in a horse barn, and reproductions of vintage 501, 505, and 646 jeans start at $154. Checking out the salespeople is good for a cue on how to wear the different styles.

The **Diesel Denim Gallery** in Soho (68 Greene St. bet. Spring and Broome Sts., Mon–Sat 11–7, Sun 12–6, 212-966-5593) features numbered denim collections made both exclusively for the Gallery by Diesel, and by fashion designers collaborating with Diesel, like Karl Lagerfeld. It is one of the few spaces in Soho that has been occupied by fashion, electronics, and even airline companies, in an effort to bridge the gap between the commercialism of the area and the creative community. The jeans are showcased singly, along a wall and a sparse few racks, and on the southern wall is a rotating art show, organized by an independent curator. Larger-than-life potted plants sit in the middle of the store. The space is more about showing artwork than it is about selling jeans. Recent shows have included Anime and Japanese pop art. The mix of art and commerce in the space highlights Diesel's funky novelty denim collection that changes from season to season. If you are interested in limited-edition denim, and have tired of the hackneyed Diesel styles walking America's streets, the Diesel Denim Gallery is a must-hit shopping spot. Most jeans start at $200.

A.P.C. (131 Mercer St. bet. Prince and Spring Sts., Mon–Sat 11–7, Sun 12-6, 212-966-9685). Owner/designer Jean Touitou sells his signature, chic, understated basics, but the reason people are addicted to A.P.C. is the denim. His signature jeans are unwashed, untreated, no-frills dark blue jeans in varying rises and lengths (none, it should be noted, go much below the bellybutton) starting at $100. The staff is Parisian-cool, but American-friendly.

What Goes around Comes Around (351 W. Broadway bet. Broome and Grand Sts., Mon–Sat 11–8, Sun 12–7, 212-343-9303) has a great selection of vintage leather, fur, Western wear, women's designer clothing, military and motorcycle collectibles, with fabulous belts and boots to match. Pricey, but could be worth it if you find the perfect pair of high-waisted jeans to sashay to the square dance in! Jeans are around $150; other accessories vary depending on vintage.

dusica dusica

❄ 67 Prince Street at Crosby Street

HOURS: Daily 11–8

PHONE: 212-966-9099

A luxurious collection of handcrafted shoes and bags for the true shoe connoisseur who has an eye for great design at a great price.

Yugoslavian designer Dusica Sacks teamed up with Aleksandra Hahn (formerly of Prada) to open this minimal Crosby Street boutique. Using soft leather and other fabrics in muted, flesh-inspired hues, the shoes are built with feminine lines and unusual details. Gathered and ruffled leather, peek-a-boo toe covers that can be worn over and under the toes, and chiffon ankle ties give the shoes a delicate and abstract quality. Dusica also specializes in cashmere boots specially treated to withstand at least the milder aspects of a New York City winter.

The handbags are unusual as well, with very little hardware to obstruct the flow of leather and fabric in each bag. Certain styles are interchangeable (you can carry it as a tote or a slouchy shoulder sack, for instance) just by bending the hidden wire in the strap, and the closures are hidden. Sacks's designs are space-mod, for women who appreciate luxurious details, but don't need status symbol logos.

The average cost of shoes is $200–250, but given the solid construction and beautiful materials, the shoes are practical and versatile enough to justify the cost.

nolita

Nolita (a hybrid moniker of "North of Little Italy") is known for its quaint buildings, leafy streets, and small boutiques. In the last ten years, the neighborhood has become a hub for younger designers and shops that carry cutting-edge clothing and accessories. However, the old-world romance of the neighborhood, once home to Martin Scorsese and other legendary Italian-American New Yorkers, remains. Most of the stores' employees embody the personality of the neighborhood—youthful, relaxed, and beautiful. Nolita combines the quality of Soho shopping with the chill vibe of the Village—without the crowds. A great part of town to grab a seat at an outdoor café and people watch, because it doesn't get prettier than this.

malia mills

❊ 199 Mulberry Street bet. Spring and Kenmare Streets
HOURS: Tu–Sun 12–7, closed Mon
PHONE: 212-625-2311
WEB: www.maliamills.com

A swimsuit boutique that makes flattering cuts for any body type in fashion-forward fabrics and unusual, fun colors.

Malia Mills has a loyal clientele who pay homage to her by buying her swimsuits every year. Malia has almost shattered the barrier between women and their bodies with her suits. It's hard to believe that liberation for women and their curves would come from a swimwear designer. Malia has made it her company's mission to take the edge off of bathing suit shopping, which is a tall order. She pulls it off by cutting flattering shapes, pushing the envelope with novel fabrications and embellishments, and creating a positive store environment. Her company's motto is "Love Thy Differences."

The store is simple—a rack of suits on the right, a long chest of drawers on the left. The staff is friendly and will find you your size, make color suggestions, and smile all the while. The dressing rooms are spacious, with room for friends to provide moral support. "We're here to make shopping for swimwear as anxiety-free and liberating as possible," says a spokesperson for Malia Mills. Suits range from $80 per piece, and up. The other cool thing about Malia Mills is that mixing and matching is encouraged, and many of the colors and fabrics complement one another. At the end of each season, the store has a great sale where you can get two for one (so, a two-piece suit for $80). Call the office or check the web site for details about the sales.

In spring 2005, look for more fun with chocolate-colored pinstripes, Swarovski crystals, and navy leather suits with light beige stitching. You're practically ready to make a cameo in that music video!

Also uptown (960 Madison Ave. bet. E. 75th and 76th Sts., Mon–Sat 10–7, 212-517-7485).

---

lace NYC

✳ 223 Mott Street bet. Spring and Prince Streets
HOURS: Tue–Sat 12–7:30, Sun 12–6, closed Mon
PHONE: 212-941-0528
WEB: www.lacenyc.com

A stylish women's shoe boutique specializing in hard-to-find European designers and styles.

A bit south of the shopping hubbub of Nolita are the intimate environs of Lace. The store's décor is coy and stylish, with 1920s floral wallpaper, a vintage trellis, a Queen Anne chair, and copper butterfly accents. A cheeky finishing touch is a framed 1970s *Cosmopolitan* cover over the mantle. "It's '70s glamour with a Victorian edge," says owner Colleen Brennan. You feel like a starlet from any era, choosing from her array of fabulous shoes that are carefully selected like a box of delectable chocolates. As a former fashion stylist and editor, her desires fulfill the shoe lover's most ardent interests—sexy shapes and novel fabrications. Lace carries exclusive, vibrant, standout styles from the best European designers, which are not available anywhere else in the city (to clarify: she chooses the one style from a line that no one else will carry, as well as strictly nondomestic designers). The result is the shoe closet every woman fantasizes about.

Her shoes are extremely feminine. Studded pumps are feminized by tri-color detailing and round toes. Other shoes have wedge heels and ankle straps. You can get your basic black shoe here, but if you have an eye for color, you will be in heaven. Lace also carries some exclusives that you may not find in department stores. Large, soft, cloudlike handbags complement the shoes, perched like Cheshire cats around the store.

Designers include Martine Sitbon, Vivienne Westwood, Moschino, Le Flesh, Gaspard Yurkievich, Etro, and Sonia Rykiel. Shoes range from $200 and up.

Shoe Doctors

Because there are so many fabulous shoes to buy in Nolita, from better-known designers like **Sigerson Morrison** (28 Prince St. bet. Mott and Elizabeth Sts., 212-219-3893) also **Sigerson Morrison Accessories** around the corner (242 Mott St. bet. Prince and E. Houston Sts., 212-941-5404) and **Edmund Castillo** (219 Mott St. bet. Prince and Spring Sts., 212-431-5320), to newcomers like **Lace NYC** and **I Heart**, an excellent cobbler nearby keeps soles intact. Head over to **Cowboy Boot Hospital** (4 Prince St. bet. Bowery and Elizabeth, Mon–Fri 9–6, Sat 10–5, 212-941-9532) where you can fix a broken heel or shape up a sole within minutes, if the cobbler isn't too busy. Prices are reasonable (under $30 a pair for most services) and you can talk him down a few dollars depending on how severe the damage is. Here are the names of some other excellent cobblers around the city; depending on what neighborhood you're in when the sidewalk gets the better of your heel:

Magic Watch and Shoe Repair (30 Carmine St. bet. Bleecker St. and 7th Ave. S., Mon–Fri 8–6:30, 212-727-2948) is the shoe equivalent of the "Soup Nazi" in *Seinfeld*. He's been known to scold customers for waiting too long to have protective Vibrim soles and heel protectors put onto their fancier shoes and boots ($25 a pair).

Alex Shoe Store (57 2nd Ave. bet. 3rd and 4th Sts., Mon–Thu 9–7, Fri and Sun 10–4, closed Sat, 212-533-9442). These proficient cobblers make platforms for shoes, fix zippers, and sell shoes, socks, and other accessories that may have gone the way of your broken heel.

Angelo's (666 5th Ave. at 53rd St., Mon–Fri 7–6:30, Sat 10–5, closed Sun, 212-757-6364). Major department stores, like Bergdorf Goodman, send their customers to Angelo's. The cobblers specialize in custom work that includes matching the fabric of shoes or handbags in order to make alterations or repairs. This includes dying shoes to match a dress. More famously, the cobblers do boot alterations, including widening with zippers, or tapering baggy knee-high leather

leather boots to fit boots to all sizes of calves. The average cost for boot alteration is $65 and up.

Shoe Service Plus (15 W. 55th St. bet. 5th and 6th Aves., Mon–Fri 7–7, Sat 10–5, 212-262-4823) is an excellent cobbler who repairs shoes and also dyes them to match, which is great for weddings and other special occasions.

Top Service (845 7th Ave., Mon–Fri 8–6, Sat 9–3, closed Sun, 212-765-3190). According to some New Yorkers, this is the best place in the city to have shoes repaired or cleaned. They have been open for fifteen years and for this level of experience are very reasonable. Cleaning costs $6–12 and repairs usually don't run over $30.

Kaufman Shoe Repair Supplies (346 Lafayette St. bet. Bond and Bleecker Sts., Sun–Fri 6:30–2, 212-777-1700). This store sells missing pieces for broken shoes—heels, tassels, ties, straps, etc.

daily 235

※ 235 Elizabeth Street bet. Prince and Houston Streets
HOURS: Mon–Sat 12–8, Sun 12–7
PHONE: 212-334-9728

An offbeat gift shop specializing in kitsch and memorabilia.

Daily 235 is a little gift shop that's tucked between two boutiques in Nolita, like a playful puppy sandwiched between a couple of serious adults. The shop has occupied this position on the block for ten years, long before Nolita was a hip shopping destination. Owner Jasmine Krause and her partner worked for Ad Hoc, a popular and revolutionary home store in Soho in the '80s that pioneered wired and industrial shelving units for the home. Such shelves are used in their store, which is a small, spare space, packed with fun toys, gift items, and memorabilia, artfully arranged to invite experimentation.

It's easy to see why the shop is so popular and has been around for so long. The reasonably priced gift items are both historically and culturally fascinating. The store is a veritable museum for random objects and memorabilia; it could be 2005 or 1920 for all you know. The owners appreciate how far a little nostalgia and lightness can go. Merchandise includes everything from gag gifts (trick cigarettes, gum, jack-in-the-boxes) to memorabilia from the '50s to comic books, toys, and lunch boxes. The nostalgic feeling in the store often gives way to modern humor, and the selection is always changing. Daily 235 is the perfect place to pick up a last-minute gift or just something fun. Prices are reasonable for the novelty and the neighborhood—you can find something neat for $3.

I Got You, Babe

Kids are little people. Sometimes they get stuck wearing something that's a bit more "appropriate" than they would prefer. Here are some shops that let the young ones reap the same benefits of the fun, varied shopping options that their parents do. From toys to T-shirts, here are a couple of the coolest babies' and kids' shops in lower Manhattan.

Dinosaur Hill (306 E. 9th St. bet. 1st and 2nd Aves. Daily 11-7, 212-473-5850). Everyone in the East Village loves this eclectic toy store, including parents and over-grown kids like me. You'll find unusual handmade marionettes from the Czech Republic dangling from the ceiling ($21–90), plus sequined wooden horses from Burma and Thailand and jack-in-the-boxes (cat-, dog-, and cow-in-the-boxes, too). They also have UGLY doll key chains, as well as a variety of stuffed animals. The store stocks many neat retro toy brands that are gratifying to see still around (like Rubik's Cubes and Erector Sets). Dinosaur Hill also gift-wraps everything on the premises, which is a huge time saver as well.

Pipsqueak (248 Mott St. bet. Prince and E. Houston Sts., Tue–Sat 11–7, Sun 12–6, 212-226-8824). A lovely clothing store for little ones, with a very reasonably priced selection from Portugal, France, Italy, England, Japan, and the U.S. Sizes go from newborn to age six, though infant sizes offer a larger selection. The DouDous make an interesting but loveable gift for a newborn—they are teddy bears made of baby-sized blanket squares.

Julian & Sara (103 Mercer St. bet. Prince and Spring Sts., Tue–Fri 11:30–7, Sat–Sun 12–6, 212-226-1989). A children's clothing store that's a bit on the pricey side, but the bonus is that while you're shopping, your little ones can play with the toys in the store, so you can browse in peace. The store carries an almost entirely European selection of clothing, with sizes ranging from infants to age twelve (although your twelve-year-old may not be so psyched about the clothes in here). Dresses are unpretentious in ecru and ivory woven fabrics ($100–250). Stop here for a special baby gift, or to indulge your newest family member with something a little extraordinary. Miniature dress shirts and slacks for boys ($100–250) are adorable.

i heart

❈ **262 Mott Street bet. Prince and Houston Streets**
HOURS: Mon–Sat 12–8, Sun 12–7
PHONE: 212-219-9265
WEB: www.iheartnyc.com

Immense store, gallery, and lounge space featuring local artwork, books, and music, amidst collections of cutting-edge women's fashion.

The precious name of this store belies the edginess of its immense subterranean space, with its seventeen-foot ceilings. Owners Antonia Kojuharova and Jill Bradshaw are veterans in New York's creative community who bring a nontraditional yet classy sensibility to their retail concept. Featuring the artwork of local designers and painters, the space is designed for comfort and play, a station on the dial of cultural frequency. The accessories, books, and CDs are displayed along the wall in glass cases and on modular shelving units, as in an art gallery. Inspiration for these ladies comes from art, color, music, and their favorite designers.

Featured clothing designers are Karen Walker, Eley Kishimoto, United Bamboo, Rachel Comey, and Ladies of the Canyon. Most of these lines come from established younger designers who cater to working people in their age group. Eley Kishimoto makes shoes, handbags, and clothing using bright colors and a combination of contrasting elements like leather and suede, or leather and perforated plastic. United Bamboo's line provides the fashionable professional with quality suiting and luxe detailing. Ladies of the Canyon, who are a bit less serious, riff on T-shirts and sweatshirts from the '80s—off the shoulder, surf-inspired graphics. There is a wide range of items, and the prices reflect this spectrum. Tops range from $40–300, bottoms $90–300, coats $150–1000, shoes $50–500, and books. CDs and other smaller gift items are $5–50.

There is a lounge area to read books, as well as a listening station to sample the latest pop/rock dance flavor of the moment. CDs also include compilations by local DJs, generally rock, rap, reggae, or disco.

Where the Music Is

A great deal of New York's cultural currency stems from the abundance of sources we have for music. Here are the best:

Other Music (15 E. 4th St., Mon–Fri 12–9, Sat 12–8, Sun 12–7, 212-477-8150, www.othermusic.com). OM carries a select canon of the classics, and stocks many local and hard-to-find labels and artists from around the world. Electronic, dub, and rock are the forte here. Staff is very knowledgeable and helpful, and the store publishes a great e-mail newsletter full of vivid details and recommendations. OM also hosts in-store appearances by some of their featured artists—check their web site for details.

Rocks in Your Head (157 Prince St., Mon–Fri 12–9, Sat 12–10, Sun 12–8, 212-475-6729). This record store specializes in indie rock music, new and rare vinyl, DVDs, and used CDs. The salespeople are stylish boys who act chilly, but are helpful when asked questions. Flipping through the records here reminds me of flipping through the card catalog at the public library—it's a bit dusty but there is also a tremendous amount of music knowledge emanating from the stacks. This is a good place to go if you know what you're looking for, and it's generally hard to find.

Etherea (66 Ave. A, Sun–Thu 12–10, Fri–Sat 12–11, 212-358-1126). In addition to a great selection of popular and alternative music, Etherea stocks good imported music magazines, like *The Wire* from the U.K. They have a good selection of popular indie artists; if you've recently read about a band, you will find them here easily, and usually in stock. I like that Etherea isn't as expensive as Other Music. Most of the CDs are under $13.

Jammyland (60 E. 3rd St., Mon–Thu 12–8, Fri–Sat 12–10, 212-614-0185, www.jammyland.com) is a Jamaican music store specializing in new, rare, and hard-to-find dub plates (a one off copy of the original acetate recording never released on vinyl), reggae, and dancehall.

Kim's Music and Video (6 St. Mark's Place, Daily 9–12, 212-598-9985). Are you asking everyone you know if they've heard of an album or movie, and no one has? Looking for the complete Kurosawa catalog? Chances are you'll find it at Kim's! The used CDs here are especially good because the store's discerning customers donate them. They also sell vinyl.

lunettes et chocolat

✳ 25 Prince Street bet. Mott and Elizabeth Streets
HOURS: Daily 11–7
PHONE: (Glasses) 212-334-8484, (Chocolate) 212-925-8800
WEB: www.selimaoptique.com, www.mariebelle.com

A specialty eyewear and chocolate boutique that combines the sophisticated spirit of two popular designers in an offbeat way.

They say you shouldn't go into business with your friends. Not so, say Mariebelle and Selima Salaun, who also live across the street from each other. Both women are successful in their own right, but they opened this whimsical Nolita boutique to celebrate two important highs in life—shopping and chocolate. It is a hot combination. Surrounded by great restaurants and cafés (Café Gitane and Café El Portal are both a block away), the store caters to an evening and after-dinner customer who sips chocolate while perusing Selima's gorgeous eyeglass frames, hats, and other accessories.

Lunettes is the first boutique to feature Mariebelle's chocolates. She is originally from Honduras and now owns another chocolate-only boutique on Broome Street in Soho (**Mariebelle**, 484 Broome St., 212-925-6999). Her chocolates also retail in larger stores nationwide. She makes her chocolates locally, with edible designs rich in color. Mariebelle's signature Aztec hot chocolate is served European-style: piping-hot in small cups that give the pleasant sensation of otherworldliness. Ask for a sample.

Selima's frames, which revolutionized fashion eyewear in the 1990s, are handcrafted in artisinal plastic in vivid hues. The shapes are Eames-inspired—fluid, quirky, and simple—and have names like Fish, Mouth, and Wing. Selima has eight boutiques in Paris, New York, and Los Angeles, and this boutique is a unique addition to her repertoire.

Eyewear

Selima Optique (84 E. 7th St., 212-260-2495, Daily 12–7:30). Selima's fabulous boutiques can be found all over the city. There must be a frame for everyone—picky or not—in her store.

Also at:

- 7 Bond St. bet. Broadway and Lafayette St., Mon–Sat 11–7, Sun 12–7, 212-677-8487.
- 59 Wooster St. at Broome St., Mon–Sat 11–8, Sun 12–7, 212-343-9490.

• 899 Madison Ave. bet. E. 72nd and 73rd Sts., Mon–Sat 10:30–7, Sun 12–6, 212-988-6690.

At **Fabulous Fanny's** (335 E. 9th St., Daily 12–8, 212-533-0637), find vintage frames from the designer who made frames for George Washington and Thomas Jefferson, as well as chic frames that the shop lends on occasion to theater and film companies involved in costume or period projects. Prices for frames vary widely depending on vintage.

Facial Index (104 Grand St. at Mercer St., Mon–Sat 11–7, Sun 12–6, 646-613-1055). This Japanese-owned store features avant-garde, modern frames from all over the world. Prices start at $260 for frames.

Morganthal Frederics (944 Madison Ave., Mon–Fri 10–7, Sat 10–6, Sun 12–6, 212-744-9444). This quintessential New York store's delicate, lace-pattern laminates and etched metals stand out from the crowd. Prices vary widely from $200 all the way up to $1000 for fourteen-carat gold frames.

cath kidston

�֍ 201 Mulberry St. bet. Spring and Broome Streets
HOURS: Mon–Thu 11–7, Fri–Sat 11–8, Sun 12–6
PHONE: 212-343-0223
WEB: www.cathkidston.com

A popular British home designer's American flagship store featuring trademark vintage prints on everything from bibs to shower curtains.

Walking into the brightly lit, colorfully merchandised U.S. flagship store for the British designer Cath Kidston is like walking into a vintage British cottage. Kidston, a household name in

England, is known for her trademark antique rose print fabrics, and the store is set up to educate the customer in British design, vintage home furnishings, and interior decorating. The store sells Kidston's quintessentially English designs, including cushions, china, bags, stationery, nightwear, T-shirts, towels, bed linen, bath soaps, candles, and children's clothing. What's fun about the store is that you can totally immerse yourself in the English style of eccentric pattern mixing. Large floral prints complement the stronger solid colors for bags and accessories, and corduroy is used for furnishings.

The store also carries the popular 1999 title by Kidston, *Vintage Style*, which instructs the reader in her signature methods and color combinations. She sells everything for the home, including bolts of fabrics for you to buy in case you are inspired to stitch a pillowcase or curtain of your own. The children's merchandise is especially fun, including sleeping bags, nursery items, bibs, and T-shirts. Prices are average; the home items cost around $40 and up, and the kids' items average $25–40.

gas bijoux

❊ 238 Mott Street bet. Prince and Spring Streets
HOURS: Daily 11–7
PHONE: 212-334-7290

A French collection of Asian-inspired costume jewelry for the woman who's not afraid of a little sparkle.

Andre Gas, a French designer who owns several boutiques in Paris and St. Tropéz, among other places, infuses his jewelry with his cosmopolitan sensibility. Atop the wooden cabinets around the perimeter of the shop are bright green silk brocade panels, elaborating on the jewelry's colonial sensibility. Gas embellishes Asian-influenced beads or coins with glass, rhinestones, or enamel, before incorporating them into his designs. His signature earring shape is the chandelier, which comes in many different colors and shapes. The jewelry has a festive, holiday feel to it, but some pieces are very Bohemian at the same time. You can wear a more elaborate piece to a wedding, or dress anything down with a T-shirt for a night of karaoke. These pieces are imaginative, feminine, and fun, and are worth a bit of a splurge ($145–215).

Street Vendors

Hundreds of different vendors line Broadway, Prince, and Spring streets (they're out year-round, but more so in the spring and summertime). You can find everything from art books, to designed matchbook covers, dolls, curios, and more. For both tourists and natives alike, street vendors are wonderful because the merchandise for sale is handmade, often one-of-a-kind craftwork that would sell for hundreds inside a shop. Buying from these vendors also differs from the more popular flea markets in the city (see **To The Market We Go**, p. 87) because at the market, the selection is carefully curated to cater to the discerning shopper.

The streets are the place to find the next big thing in jewelry and crafts design, as many young designers do not have the means to produce their lines commercially. Urban Outfitters will charge you $30 for a pair of earrings you can find (better-made) from one of these vendors for $5. Shopping these vendors is a good way to support local artists who have built up a thriving outdoor retail community in Soho by establishing outdoor retail spaces. Many of them have been in the same licensed location for years. A random sampling of permanent vendors (there are many) include:

There is a vendor on Prince Street who sells round, ample, hand-knit/crocheted, nubby hats, and ponchos ($25 and up).

You can buy art, architecture, and photography coffee table books on Prince Street. Titles from Taschen, Phaidon Press, and others sell for ten to thirty percent below market value.

Cleo Van Elton, a jewelry designer and vendor who sits on the corner of Prince and Broadway, designs earrings and necklaces using papier–mâché with gold overlay, semi-precious stones with sterling silver, and gold-plated sterling silver. Her styles are very feminine and always on trend ($15–100).

The T-shirt peddler on Prince between Broadway and Mercer is also a veteran of the Soho vendor scene. He screen-prints old movie logos, rock bands, funny sayings, and more, onto American Apparel T-shirts. His claim to fame is a "Jesus is my homeboy" shirt, which is for sale in retail stores as well. His T's go for $11 apiece (which is a steal in an oversaturated T-shirt market) but you can negotiate if you are buying more than one.

There are hand-painted matchbooks available right outside of **Mercer Kitchen** restaurant, at the corner of Greene and Prince Streets.

Along West Broadway between East Houston and Canal, you can find many street artists producing original paintings, charcoal drawings, watercolors, and sketches, as well as vendors selling photographs. It's quite possible to find a nice piece of original artwork here for under $100.

zero maria cornejo

❊ 225 Mott Street bet. Prince and Spring Streets
HOURS: Mon–Fri 1–8, Sat–Sun 12:30–6:30
PHONE: 212-925-3849
WEB: www.mariacornejo.com

Luxe fabrics and elegant, simply designed clothing for style mavens of all ages.

Like its name, Zero starts from the beginning, building elegant, functional pieces from minimal designs. The clothing is in geometric, imaginative shapes in Southwestern taupes, creams, and grays. The clothing would look good on anyone from a dancer to a woman who is several months pregnant. Capelets, ponchos, wide-leg trousers, pleated skirts, and dresses fill out Maria Cornejo's versatile collection. On her web site are photographs of the current season's line, which will give you a better sense of her aesthetic.

The Chilean-born designer pays a great deal of attention to details and draping of fabric. The idea is to easily incorporate any of her unusual pieces into your everyday wardrobe. Contrast is key to her design; she uses prints with solids, and sharp tailoring with fluent contour. The fabrics are unusual and of high quality, like viscose jersey, silk charmeuse, Scottish wool, French herringbone wool, African jacquards, indigo denim, organic cotton sweatshirt, silk cashmere, and shiny lamé. Cornejo also features a bridge collection (a line of clothing that's a lower-priced version of its designer collection; for example, DKNY for Donna Karan) made of fleece that includes wraps and cardigans.

Cornejo originally opened the space in 1997 to join the movement of independent designers in New York who use small design studios to manufacture and sell their own lines. Zero is sold at Barney's New York, but the Nolita shop is a cool gray pond compared to the chaos of midtown Manhattan. The space is gallery-like, and the clothing feels like wearable art.

Prices are on the higher side, but for basics like trousers and sweaters, Zero outshines more traditional brands, like Ralph Lauren. It is nice to be able to wear a plain piece that isn't completely predictable but looks elegant. You can buy a T-shirt for $49; pants are generally between $189–289; tops can go anywhere from $189–395 depending on the fabric; coats will run from $600–900; and the lower-end fleece collection sells for between $196–240.

polux fleuriste

❈ 248 Mott Street bet. Prince and Houston Streets
HOURS: Mon–Sat 10–7, closed Sun
PHONE: 212-219-9646

Flowers from all over the world are transformed into French country-style, artistic arrangements for delivery.

Audrey Tatou loading her bicycle up with wine and flowers on her way home in *Amelie* is enviably representative of the average citizen's life in Paris. Polux owner Anoushka Levy, a Parisian, says she wanted to recreate her hometown's romanticism here in New York. Her flower shop, next door to her husband's superb restaurant, Café Gitane, is French down to the very last detail. Her exquisite flower collection comes from all over the world—the Netherlands, Israel, and South America, for starters.

The inside of the store is cool and tiled, and was custom designed to feel like a Parisian shop. Levy has incorporated a lifestyle element into the boutique, and sells such items as handmade teacups and bowls, loose teas, candles, marmalade, and dolls made from vintage fabrics ($20 and up).

The minimum for delivery is $75, but if you visit the store, you can find an arrangement for any price you wish (though it may be small if you go too low). Polux also incorporates vintage elements into its arrangements, such as an eighteenth-century vase, jars from the 1940s, and vintage fabrics. With a delivery, Polux includes lovely handmade details in the packaging, like a wax "Polux" seal on the leaf of the flower, a handmade cookie, and flower food that is attached to a small illustrated pamphlet on how to care for them. It is sweet down to the very last touch. Anoushka's sentiment about bringing us the good life is infectious.

While You're There. . .

You may want to walk further south into Chinatown to **Golden City Floral Arts** (221 Centre Street, Mon–Fri 9:30–6, Sat–Sun 9:30–7:30, 212-219-0235) where they have gorgeous orchids, lilies, and tulips for very reasonable prices. They also do decent arrangements quite cheaply, and the old woman who works in here is so charming that the whole experience is very pleasant.

To the Flower Market We Go

Manhattan's flower district can be intimidating to the first timer, but here are a few shops to check out. Another great way to shop in New York is to shop the districts—generally, they are one city block of different stores selling different varieties of the same item. If you have the cash and want flowers for decoration, the selection is exquisite. The Flower District is, roughly, on West 28th Street between 6th and 7th Avenues—some stores spill onto 6th Avenue as well. Between the hours of 7 and 9 a.m., the shops are filled with stylists, decorators, and designers fiercely competing over the best varieties of flowers available, so don't expect the vendors to be very helpful if you want to buy a lily for your office desk. However, if you go in the middle of the day, you can certainly choose flowers to your liking that are much nicer than what you will find at your neighborhood deli.

There are stores that specialize in different varieties of flowers—from tropical to country flowers, to grasses. Here are several stores in the Flower District worth checking out. They are all markets, and as such the selection changes on a daily basis. They are, however, the largest in the District, so you are sure to find what you are looking for at any one of them:

Fischer & Page Ltd. (134 W. 28th St. bet. 6th and 7th Aves., Mon–Sun 6–11, Sat opens a little earlier and closes a bit later depending on business, 212-645-4106).

Associated Cut Flower Company, Inc. (118 W. 28th St. bet. 6th and 7th Aves., 212-367-7805).

US Evergreen (805 6th Ave., Mon–Fri 5–1:30, Sat 6–1, 212-741-5300).

red flower

❊ 13 Prince Street bet. Bowery and Elizabeth
HOURS: Tu–Sun 12–7, closed Mon
PHONE: 212-966-5301
WEB: www.redflower.com

When you don't want a run-of-the-mill vanilla candle, Red Flower carries comfort items in specially formulated fragrances from all over the world.

From the great airline-inspired logo to the relaxing dark environs of its Nolita location, Red Flower promises to provide a very cool experience. Yael Alkalay and Victor Silviera, childhood friends who traveled the world over, have put together a collection of soaps, lotions, teas, and candles that give off exotic scents from every corner of the globe. The products are superior because of the purity of fragrance, the simple, elegant packaging, and the fantastic customer service you get when you visit the store. They serve Red Flower's jasmine tea, which you can sip through a *bombilla*, a metal straw with a round perforated bulb at the bottom, from Argentina (also for sale, $20).

Celebrity patronage is in no short order here, as Madonna swears by the Spanish Gardenia, R&B singer Usher by the Italian Blood Orange, and rumor has it that P. Diddy only burns Himalayan Larch candles in his Manhattan offices.

Prices range from $18–32, making a stop at Red Flower perfect for a gift or for a self-indulgent treat.

Yoga

Some of us indulge in a spiritual massage after a long day of shopping, and inside many of the buildings in lower Manhattan are yoga studios packed with women and men of all ages. Fortunately, most studios offer classes frequently, are not terribly expensive, and offer additional services like massage, fresh food and juices, and more.

Atmananda Yoga & Holistic Spa (552 Broadway, Yoga 212-625-1511, Holistic Spa 212-625-8559). Atmananda is known for its teacher-training institute, but it also features a food and drink bar where raw food dishes are featured. Massage, facials, and waxes are offered, as well. Classes include the Ayangar style of yoga, which is a slow and detailed practice that involves getting your postures and movements absolutely correct while focusing on special muscle groups. Classes cost $16 and the second class is free, or you can buy multiple classes on a card.

Jivamukti (404 Lafayette St. bet. Astor Place and E. 4th St., 3rd floor, 212-353-0214 and 800-295-6814). Probably the most "celebrity-fied" yoga center in the city, Madonna used to frequent this popular studio. Classes here may be more crowded but the instruction is superb. $17 for a single class.

Bikram Yoga NYC (797 8th Ave., 212-245-2525, several locations in almost all the major neighborhoods of Manhattan, see www.bikramyoganyc.com for details). Bikram is the "hot" style of yoga, where the air-tight room is heated up to 100 degrees to allow for optimal stretching conditions. Price is $20 for a single class, although you can go to unlimited classes the first week for the same $20.

lower east side

Most walking tours of the Lower East Side will begin in front of the famous **Katz's Deli** (205 E. Houston at the corner of Ludlow St., 212-254-2246). Katz's is an institution that's seen the scene move from hard to hip in the last ten years; the restaurant has hosted meetings of gangsters as well as the famous orgasm scene in *When Harry Met Sally*. Today, the Lower East Side is filled with nice boutiques, restaurants, and cafés, but the gritty character remains. Some new businesses have tried to assimilate to the neighborhood by leaving storefronts intact—others, like the gargantuan Surface Hotel on Rivington Street, have not. Street art and old-school businesses are still plentiful. The Lower East Side remains a vibrant cultural center for young New Yorkers as well as the Latin community. Hungry? If you walk east to **Clinton Street**, you are sure to find some of the best dining in the city.

foley and corinna men

❊ 143 Ludlow Street bet. Stanton and Rivington
   HOURS: Mon–Fri 1–8, Sat–Sun 12–8
   PHONE: 212-529-5043

   A men's boutique specializing in a mix of formal, casual, and evening wear for a downtown customer.

Foley and Corinna Men is part of a shopping revolution for men in the city. Instead of merchandising their clothing separately, they display clothes intuitively—all mixed up. Suits are next to rock 'n' roll T-shirts (around $30); new and vintage shirts are hanging on the same rack; and denim is shown with everything. Foley and Corinna's men's line consists mostly of loose, comfortable, button-down shirts, T-shirts, and restructured vintage pants. Today's man isn't looking for a quick fix—he's just as element-oriented as the most discerning woman is. If you know a guy with an eye for vintage, this is the place to take him. Most T-shirts run around $25. The in-house label items, featuring well-cut trousers (about $150) and stripe-free button-downs in imaginative prints ($100–125) are definitely worth the price.

The owners, Dana Foley and Anna Corinna, opened this boutique after the success they were enjoying with their women's new and vintage clothing boutique around the corner (**Foley and Corinna**, 108 Stanton St., 212-529-2388). The clothes, designed by Foley under a label of the same name, are sexy, and have names like Harlow and Jayne Mansfield. Tops that double as dresses, corseted tops, and pants are for sale here, as well as some of the best vintage clothing and shoes in the area. The trousers, which Foley is known for, are low-rise men's pants that have a leather D-ring belt attached. There are also Indian-inspired tops in bright colors if you're a fan of cool, gauzy, drapey, embroidered stuff. Tops and bottoms range from $200–300. Corinna designs jewelry made from pieces of necklaces that have been deconstructed and put back together. The handbags are '80s inspired with oversized sequined patches and flowered embellishments, sometimes doubled up.

Tailors

A great tailor can be a magician; a Salvation Army suit can become Brit pop glamour. Even the White House has called on the services of the same tailor for over thirty years, and England's Savile Row is world famous. From buttoned-up to Bohemian, New York's tailors cater to a broad range of tastes and styles with low to high-end custom services.

Ignacio Tailor (119 E. 60th St. bet. Park and Lexington Aves., 2nd floor, Mon–Fri 9–7, Sat 9–3, 212-758-2747). All of the shops on upper Madison Avenue send their customers to Ignacio, and his alterations, particularly for pants, either resizing or taking up, are excellent. Pant hems average $15, altering a dress or jacket starts at around $40.

New York is probably the only city where you can find full businesses running out of extremely small spaces, all over the Lower East Side, Chinatown, and Nolita. **Victor and Jose Tailor** (205 Mott St. bet. Spring and Broome Sts., Mon–Sat 11–8, 212-941-0348) whip up a solid pant hem for $5. That's right—no more and no less. Something complicated, like altering a fully beaded top, will cost you about half of what an uptown tailor would charge ($30).

À la bazaar tailors in Hong Kong, India, and Morocco, there are New York tailors who will duplicate designer suits. Give them the suit you like, and the fabric, and they will copy it stitch for stitch, made to measure. **LNK Custom Tailoring** (178 Mulberry St. bet. Broome and Kenmare Sts., Mon–Sat 11–8, Sun by appointment, 212-226-7755) will make you any suit you like for $700. If you add in the value of his being at your beck and call, you could end up getting more than you bargained for.

casa de rodriguez

✻ 156 Stanton Street bet. Suffolk and Clinton Streets
HOURS: Daily 12–7
PHONE: 212-995-8880
WEB: www.casaderodriguez.com

Jody and David Rodriguez make beautiful, highly wearable, fashion-forward hats.

In the past, Casa de Rodriguez has retailed at major department stores like Barney's, but the neighborhood is lucky to have this little Lower East Side boutique. "We've always been a little ahead of our time," Jody told me. "That's what it takes when you are wearing hats; you are at the forefront of fashion." Indeed, I felt each hat in the shop could have transformed not only my appearance, but my outlook, as well. The oversized berets are ultra-mod, French on the back of a Vespa. The fur newsboy hats are cute and practical, for New York winter shopping excursions. The details in the lining and embellishments are what make these hats stand out—the rings fabricated from different materials, the soft suede bands around the brims, and the unique fabrics.

"You can come in and buy a hat and put it in the closet for a couple of years, and then take it out and feel very confident about wearing it," Jody says. Each hat has a classic shape, but with a modern twist that makes it fun. Casa de Rodriguez also does custom hat design and fittings—just ask. Hats range in price from $75–750.

Hats

Yes, it's true, hats are for trendsetters, and here is a list of shops that will get your head ready for any season or reason.

Eugenia Kim (203 E. 4th St. bet. Aves. A and B, Mon–Fri 10–8, Sat 12–8, Sun 1–6, 212-673-9787). Eugenia Kim has been selling her collectible hats to quirky fashionistas for years. Her hats sell at **Barney's Co-op** (pg. 99), **Auto** (pg. 85), and other boutiques in the city. She is known for her playful fabrics and shapes, which can be dressed up or down. In 2004, she stepped into the world of shoe design, and garnered praise for her exciting new shoe collection, which combines her playful sensibility with fun, stylish, and feminine design. A great example is a brightly colored pump with a chrome heel, and a rabbit fur-trimmed teal ankle boot.

The Village Scandal (19 E. 7th St. bet. 2nd and 3rd Aves., Mon–Sat 12 noon–midnight, Sun 1–11, 212-460-9358). Retro hats are the look here. Milliners like the San Francisco Hat Company lend a snazzy collection of newsboy, fedora, and other assorted classic hat shapes, in different fabrications (tweed, leather, fur, silk, etc.), to the mix. The proof is in the details—real ostrich feathers, crocodile trim, and lace. Handbags and other accessories (brooches, earrings, necklaces, and more) are also worth a peek. Open until midnight most days, for those last minute fashion turnabouts. Hats run between $25–500.

Forward (72 Orchard St. bet. Broome and Grand Sts., Daily 12–7, 646-264-3233). Forward is what is known as an incubator for young designers—the store sells their lines and teaches them about the fashion business. At Forward, the accessories, in particular, are stellar, and the hats are worth making the trip south of Delancey for. Prices change constantly based on the season's chosen designers.

Lisa Shaub (232 Mulberry St., Wed 12–5, Thu 12–7, Fri 4–7, Sat 12–7, Sun 1–6, 212-965-9176). Lisa Shaub makes jewel toned, 1920s- and 30s-inspired fedoras, cloches (a type of curved hat), berets, and more in felt, velvet, and other opulent fabrics that mold to your head marvelously. Her hats make you look more glamorous than you do in that dream where you're a nightclub singer à la Billie Holiday. She also does custom. Her hats start at around $150. Lisa also sells evening bags, scarves, sarongs, straw beach bags, and feather headpieces.

edith and daha

✳ 104 Rivington Street bet. Essex and Ludlow Streets
HOURS: Mon–Fri 1–8, Sat–Sun 12–8
PHONE: 212-979-9992

A virtual warehouse of hundreds of well-edited women's clothing items and shoes.

The windows at this basement-level shop tickle the fashion itch—usually a hot dress, bag, and shoes are irresistibly on display. Edith and Daha is the mecca for vintage shoes and handbags from every era. Open for three years, the shop's popularity has spread almost strictly through word of mouth from here to Tokyo. You can find vintage for any occasion here, whether it's going to a rodeo, taking a drive through the country, or attending the Costume Gala at the Metropolitan Museum of Art. Edith Machinist and Sarah Daha have created a permanent indoor flea market, with the merchandise spilling off the racks and shoes lining the floor like they are going out of style—which technically, they once did, but now who's cashing in?

"We are interested in finding things that have style on their own, versus buying strictly designers," Edith told me.

There are still plenty of vintage Armani dresses, YSL blazers, and Gucci purses to die for. Next time you are looking for something pretty to offset your Gap jeans, look no further than the gems these ladies have dug up for you. Prices range from $25 and up.

Sweet Candy

The sweet tooth usually rears its head when you're on a shopping high, and there are several spots in the Lower East Side that will feed the beast. In fact, these are some of the premier sweet spots in Manhattan, and part of the reason the neighborhood is more of a destination than ever.

When you're done picking a rainbow of handbags and shoes at Edith and Daha, stop by **Economy Candy** (108 Rivington St., Sun–Fri 9–6, Sat 10–5, 212-254-1531) next door and get a sugar fix from any variety of candy ever made. The store has been a neighborhood fixture for over thirty years. You can find gummy anything your heart desires, a wide international variety of chocolates and caramels, kitschy wrapped candies (gummy, popping, or blue, it's all here!), and treats from your childhood, as well as a variety of other sweets, teas, and sundries.

Just up the street is the **Sugar Sweet Sunshine Bakery** (126 Rivington St., Mon–Thu 8–10, Fri 8–11, Sat 10–11, Sun 10–7, 212-995-1960) where the atmosphere is relaxed and the air is sweet. Cupcakes are the specialty, and the two always-present bakers take suggestions from their customers for recipes they grew up with. Look for red velvet with satin vanilla butter cream, pumpkin (instead of carrot cake) with cream cheese icing, lemon with lemon butter cream, yellow cake with almond butter cream (called "Bob" because it's all American), and chocolate on chocolate (called "Ooey-gooey"). They also bake cakes to order and feature other sweets like mini-cheesecakes and brownies.

Il Laboratorio del Gelato (95 Orchard St., Daily 10–6, 212-343-9922). Opened by Jon Snyder, the founder and creator of Ciao Bella, the shop is located across the street from the **Lower East Side Tenement Museum** (pg. 78), and next door to one of two rival pickle stands. The space resembles a spotless, ultra-chic lab with staff in white coats, busy perfecting a batch of gelato. A small freezer in the front advertises the twelve flavors rotated daily, so each day brings something new. In all, there are at least 75 flavors available, including cinnamon, coconut, papaya, as well as more standard flavors (sometimes). Doors close promptly at 6, so a visit is a good ending to a weekday afternoon of shopping.

Chikalicious (203 E. 10th St., Wed–Sun 3–11:30, no reservations, 212-995-9511), which is a bit further north in the East Village, is a famous dessert-only restaurant, featuring a sushi-style, à la carte dessert bar. Offerings include a three-course prix fixe menu, consisting of an "amuse" (appetizer), entree dessert, and assorted petit fours for $12, and $7 more for wine pairings.

miele

❊ 159 1/2 Ludlow Street bet. Stanton and Rivington Streets

HOURS: Tu–Sat 1–8, Sun 1–7

PHONE: 212-475-9240

"Miele" is Italian for honey, and this sweet little clothing store is great for finding unusual and hard-to-find newer clothing designers.

Miele occupies a neat, narrow space, akin to a corridor, which owner Jennifer Dutka stocks with pieces that jump out at you from the racks. She stocks trendier designers, but pays close attention to quality and finishing, which is what sets her apart from neighboring boutiques. A former buyer for other chic small boutiques, Jennifer is a great person to entrust your wardrobe makeover to. She carries New York designer Christopher Deane, who makes sophisticated silk separates with interesting details, and Australians Sass and Bide, as well as flat, tall, suede boots by Australian designers Kägi and Kristen Lee. The store also carries windbreakers and jeans by Judi Rosen, who owns **The Good, the Bad, and the Ugly** (437 E. 9th St., 212-473-3769). Feminine, flirty, fun dresses and separates round out her collection. Other designers include C. Ronson and Indigo People. It's difficult to leave without trying something on.

Jennifer describes her shop as catering to a younger woman who's becoming an adult—a teen, or someone just out of college. Indeed young celebrities have already solicited Jennifer's expertise. "No more stripes," she says, "but I still like to have fun."

bocage

❊ 177 Orchard Street bet. Stanton and Rivington Streets
HOURS: Tu–Sun 12–7
PHONE: 212-979-2909
WEB: www.bocagenewyork.com

Bocage is a crafts store that specializes in vintage and specialty materials for the modern-day hobbyist.

For the design-obsessed and the creatively handicapped alike comes this novel Lower East Side shop. Owner Stephanie Kheder has an infectious enthusiasm for collecting objects and trinkets. She stocks everything from novelty patches, appliqués, handmade pincushions, stamps (fleur de lis, anchors), and fruit erasers with satin leaves, and more. There are mosaic kits, buttons, beads, and buckles galore. The disco beads and jade flowers, as well as kits to make and embellish accessories, will help you personalize anything from clothing to paper. She also offers dill buttons—high-quality novelty buttons from Germany packaged in tubes, like candy. The designs range from colorful plastic fruit, to engraved wood, and ever-popular rhinestones, which are great for changing the look of an old blazer. The best thing about this store is that anything you choose is going to be funky and cool, whatever your purpose is.

Prices range widely, from 50 cents for ribbon, to $15 for a Bakelite button. Vintage beads, brass stampings, and most little glass and plastic embellishments start at 35 cents to $15 each. Bead stacks and jewelry kits are $14–$36. Appliqués handmade with new and vintage materials are $6–$16 depending on size and embellishments. A variety of pincushions, like handmade Bocage strawberry-shaped ones, wrist corsages, and vintage varieties are $18–200. Vintage belt buckles cost between $6–65. Typography rubber stamp sets are very popular, priced $10–18. Stephanie's sensibility is very natural and fun, and it comes through in the merchandise. "I've been able to present crafting in a more current manner, using more sophisticated imagery, which caters to a modern lifestyle," she says. She offers both group and individual classes on different aspects of crafting. Check her web site for details. "Everybody should be sharing and inspired off of each other. It's ten times more fun that way," Stephanie says. "I can make samples, products, and the products you use to make those things—none of it sells more than the other." Bocage is a well-edited playground of art materials for anyone interested in tapping their creative juices.

Trimmings, Trinkets, and More

Perhaps you have an earring that's missing a bead, or you've picked up a fabulous choker missing a rhinestone at the **Chelsea Flea Market** (pg. 88) the previous weekend. There are plenty of places you can visit to have your jewelry added onto or fixed, and you can have as much or as little involvement as you choose.

Toho Shoji (990 Avenue of the Americas bet. W. 36th and 37th Sts., Mon–Fri 9–7, Sat 10–6, Sun 10–5, 212-868-7466, www.tohoshojiny.com). This longstanding jewelry components store has been in the garment district for over twenty years. Toho Shoji sells plating, ornaments, binding, beads, silver chains, and much more, individually or wholesale.

Beads of Paradise (16 E. 17th St. bet. Broadway and 5th Ave., Daily 11–7:30, 212-620-0642). You can go here to have any jewelry finds altered or fixed. You can find beads and crafts from other countries as well. There are vials of colored beads ($3.50) everywhere in this tiny, brightly colored shop and, for the superstitious, notes on which stones will bring power, love, or luck. If you don't know what to do with the myriad objects, sign up for a weekend crash course in jewelry making ($55–75).

Artistic Ribbon, Inc. (22 W. 21st St. bet. 5th and 6th Aves., Mon–Fri 8–4, 212-255-4224, www.artisticribbon.com). Artistic Ribbon sells every kind of ribbon imaginable—solids, stripes, dots, jacquard, silk, satin, etc.—at wholesale prices only, which makes it very affordable ($7–10 for 100 yards of most varieties). Visit their web site or their offices for a catalog.

Another great ribbon shop is **So-Good** (28 W. 38th St., Mon–Fri 9–5, 212-398-0236) where you can buy beautiful grosgrain, and other ribbon at any length for a very reasonable price.

360 toy group

✳ 239 Eldridge Street bet. East Houston and
Stanton Streets
HOURS: Daily 1–7
PHONE: 646-602-0138
WEB: www.360toygroup.com

A gallery and retail store that showcases toys by leading vinyl toy designers from around the world such as Futura, Michael Lau, Eric So, Kaws, Bounty Hunter, and more.

Long popular in Asia, vinyl toys, like graphic novels, have rapidly become a part of the American vocabulary. 360 Toys was at the forefront of the vinyl and collectible toy movement in the city back in 1999, and continues to be a crossroads for people interested in collecting and making toys, as well as learning more about the art form. Toys fill glass cases and shelves along the walls in the small store space. Many local artists and neighborhood friends hang out here, especially on a nice day. This laid-back atmosphere underpins the store's philosophy. "My shop is not retail focused; it is a gallery space where people come to see more about this art form. It's warm and personal," Jakuan, the owner, says.

Jakuan opened 360 Toys to display his own artwork, and eventually began selling toys by his favorite designers as well. Soon, stores like Kid Robot in Soho and Toy Tokyo in the East Village followed suit on the retail end of the New York vinyl toy scene. Jakuan was quoted in a *New York Times* magazine profile of Michael Lau, a famous Chinese toy designer, as one of the foremost American experts on vinyl toy design. If you are interested in toy culture, graffiti art, and comic books, a visit to 360 Toy Group is essential.

Kubricks, collectible Japanese block figures that are like American Lego characters, are $5. Some toys can cost as much as $1500, like multiple figure sets of the characters in the Kurosawa film "Seven Samurai" and the three-piece Beastie Boys set ($1,200). Jakuan also sells accessories like camouflage-printed headphones ($90) for real people and mini sneakers for any action figure (G.I. Joe, Ken, etc.) by Nike, Adidas, New Balance, and more ($10). Books and magazines from all over Asia run from $20–200, like the Japanese magazine Relax or Michael Lau's book of figures.

Galleries, etc. on the Lower East Side

LES galleries, in particular, feature newer, up-and-coming artists, and are worth swinging by if you are up for a little diversion while you are shopping in the neighborhood. What's cool about these spaces is the surrounding environment. Often, gallery hopping in Chelsea, New York's current art hub, can be daunting, unpleasant, and overbearing, mostly because Chelsea is located in a far western reach of Manhattan. Since the LES is more low-key in general, popping into a gallery while shopping in the neighborhood is much more manageable.

Rivington Arms (102 Rivington St. bet. Ludlow and Essex Sts., Wed–Fri 11–6, Sat–Sun 12–6, also by appointment, 646-654-3213). The gallery features photography, painting, and installations that range in scope from politics to popular culture.

At the **Reed Space** (151 Orchard St., Daily 1–7, 212-253-0588, www.thereedspace.com), which is actually more of a store than a gallery, you can find the latest in media, technology, graphic design, and fashion street wear. Opened by Staple Design, the idea is to display the intersection between communications, art, and pop culture. There are some limited-edition books, sneakers, and toys here.

The cutely named **Cuchifritos**, located inside the **Essex Street Food Market** (120 Essex St. bet. Delancey and Rivington Sts., Daily 10–5, 212-598-4124) is the gallery arm of the Artists Alliance, Inc., a downtown art initiative devoted to public space, community, and social issues. The market, by the way, is a great place to pick up an inexpensive snack, fresh juice, fruits, or vegetables.

Maccarone, Inc. (45 Canal St. bet. Ludlow and Orchard Sts., Wed–Sun 12–6, 212-431-4977) is a relatively new gallery that features the work of young European photographers and video artists, among other exciting things.

Lastly, there is the **Lower East Side Tenement Museum** (97 Orchard St., Mon–Fri 11–5:30, Sat–Sun 10:45–5:30). The building is available through guided tour only and themed tours of the neighborhood are given daily. Check the web site at www.tenement.org for more information. It's neat to walk through the streets and see the ghosts of people past in one of New York's most historically rich neighborhoods.

For a snack, check out **Brown** (61 Hester St. bet. Grand and Canal Sts., 212-254-9825). Lunch items range from $5.50–9.50. Located a few blocks from the Lower East Side Tenement Museum, the menu features a variety of organic sandwiches, salads, and soups. Also great for sipping something hot or cold.

eggplant

�֍ 85A Orchard Street bet. Canal and Division Streets
HOURS: Mon–Fri 10–6, Sat 1–5, Sun 10–6
PHONE: 212-334-4342
WEB: www.eggplantgifts.com

Like the deep purple vegetable it is named after, Eggplant is a down-to-earth gift shop featuring items of handmade elegance.

Owner Debbie Grogan lovingly creates homemade potpourri satchels, pillows of varying shapes and sizes, handmade soaps, and other rustic items. Every object is simply designed and infused with nostalgia. Located on the border between the Lower East Side and Chinatown, this shop is just big enough to house a few of each item she makes, and the selection changes every week. The space is quiet, with iron

racks built along the walls, and two facing wrought-iron metal benches at the center of the store. It is peaceful and full of things you might see at your grandmother's house or at a country fair. Eggplant also carries paintings and sculptures by local artists. Prices vary widely, but are very reasonable for their uniqueness. Eggplant also ships worldwide.

doyle & doyle

�֍ 189 Orchard Street bet. East Houston and Stanton Streets
HOURS: Tu–Sun 1–7, Thu 1–8, closed Mon
PHONE: 212-677-9991
WEB: www.doyledoyle.com

An education in fine estate and antique jewelry.

Stores like this one, where the jewelry sells in the tens of thousands, offset the Lower East Side's grungy reputation. The jewelry is ethereal and otherworldly. Sisters Pam and Elizabeth Doyle are both trained gemologists, each having a different background. They found common ground when they opened the shop in 2000 to showcase an inventory of antique and vintage pieces they handpicked from estates. The Doyle & Doyle estate and antique jewelry collection includes pieces from the Georgian, Victorian, Edwardian, Art Nouveau, Art Deco, and Retro periods. They also have a contemporary pri-vate label collection that reflects these sensibilities. The Doyles think about color and its relationship to emotion in their design, as well as imbuing their design with some of the historical meaning certain shapes, stones, and pieces have had in the past. If you are looking for something special for a wedding, for instance, or other special occasion, the jewelry here is to die for.

Jewelry Repair

These are a couple of spots in Manhattan that are highly recommended for jewelry repair, especially trickier jobs:

Silver World (126 Macdougal St. bet. W. 3rd and Bleecker Sts., Mon–Fri 1–9, Sat–Sun 1–11, 212-358-8747) is an old-school jewelry repair store in Soho where simple mistakes are fixed on the premises, and more complicated ones are tenderly resolved within a fortnight.

Metalliferous (34 W. 46th St. bet. 5th and 6th Aves., Mon–Fri 8:30–6, Sat 10–3, 212-944-0909). Metal-liferous is a full-service, fully stocked supplier of metal, tools, and supplies to jewelers, crafters, hobbyists, met-alworkers, sculptors, and everyone else interested in metalworking and jewelry. The store features classic antique tools, discounted and used jewelry parts, and other rare finds. So if you want to add a lightning bolt charm to that Tiffany bracelet....

miks

�֎ 100 Stanton Street bet. Orchard and Ludlow Streets
HOURS: Daily 12–7:30
PHONE: 212-505-1982

A twist on casual wear and basics.

Mitsuyo Toyota, the designer at Miks, utilizes mod shapes and graphic design to inform her casual clothing collection, which is basic but fun. The collection consists of staple tops and bottoms with twists on the shape, seams, colors, and details. In particular if you are looking for an alternative to casual clothing, Toyota does a great job of making well designed, affordable separates, like a striped tank top, a shawl-collar sweatshirt, and cool T-shirts. Toyota's pants are straight cut and varied through her use of tweeds and primary-colored fabrics. Miks's appeal is in its universality—you are just as likely to find a hip kid shopping in here as someone a bit more conservative who's looking for a lift in her wardrobe. If Old Navy commercials and "office casual" are driving you up the wall, pay Miks a visit.

Tops are $80, sweaters go up to $160, skirts and pants are $130, limited edition Converse sneakers are $88, and coats and jackets are $280.

greenwich village/ meatpacking district

For New York City, Greenwich Village is generally regarded as a deeply historical and significant neighborhood. A stroll through the Village can be breathtaking, particularly the brownstones and tree-lined streets. There are hundreds of cafés, artisinal shops, galleries, and historic sites to visit. In recent years, the "good life" spread a bit further north to the Meatpacking District, a city hotspot bustling with shops, restaurants, bars, and hotels. Meatpacking stores are ideal for finding superb design ideas and objects for the home. A walk through the Village and the Meatpacking District is a delightful contrast to the senses, with shops hiding in corners where you least expect them.

flight 001

❋ 96 Greenwich Avenue bet. West 12th and Jane Streets
HOURS: Mon–Fri 11–8:30, Sat 11–8, Sun 12–6
PHONE: 212-691-1001
WEB: www.flight001.com

A hip travel store featuring the latest in luggage and gadgets for making travel as fun as can be.

Let's face it—traveling, and especially getting out of New York City, can be difficult. May as well make it fun! Flight 001's New York store looks like a neatly packed suitcase of cutting-edge travel and lifestyle accessories. Whether you are off for the weekend or traveling around the world, you will feel like one of the Avengers as you sweep through the airport terminal in your future-retro glory. Everything at Flight 001 is designed to look fabulous while making your life utterly convenient. On board, your Salsa Cabin luggage will automatically compress itself to accommodate storage, and pop right back into shape once you land. While in the air, you can stay moisturized and fresh with specially formulated skin care products by Dr. Hauschka. Once you land, you can pop your puppy out of his carrying case and consolidate him, your ID, cell phone, and keys onto an L.A. leash. Flight 001 also has its own line of products, including carrying cases for toiletries, documents, and shoes. The store carries Hobo and Jack Spade Wallets, Pan Am, Orla Kiely, Tumi luggage, and accessories. There is also a boutique in Los Angeles, San Francisco, and uptown at Henri Bendel's department store. The great thing about Flight 001 is that you don't have to sacrifice design for functionality with these products.

Potions, Lotions, and Pills

Kiehl's (109 3rd Ave. bet. 13th and 14th Sts., Mon–Sat 10–7, Sun 12–6, 212-677-3171) reopened in the East Village last year after undergoing renovations. A New York institution, Kiehl's continues to innovate in its formulations of luxurious beauty products for the face, body, and hair. Newer lines include the popular Abyssine line, which uses deep-sea extractions to cure dry skin, and Lycopene line, which uses tomatoes, an excellent antioxidant and natural sun protectant. Even classic items like Kiehl's Lip Balm are being reinterpreted in new tinted versions. Kiehl's offers three free samples of any other product when you buy something, which is where their in-house philosophy—try before you buy—comes in to great effect. They are always expanding their men's products, as well as having recently expanded into some basic cosmetics. Super-friendly service makes this New York institution well worth a visit.

C.O. Bigelow Apothecary (414 6th Ave. and W. 9th, Mon–Fri 7:30–9, Sat 8:30–7, Sun 8:30–5:30, 212-533-2700, www.bigelowchemists.com) has been an institution in Greenwich Village for over 150 years, and features an eclectic assortment of toiletries, including scissors, brushes, mirrors, and more, as well as other unrelated feminine necessities, such as beaded evening bags. Bigelow's also offers homeopathic remedies that can be mail ordered and shipped.

It's difficult to leave **Whole Body** (260 7th Ave. and 25th St., Daily 9–9, 212-924-9972) without spending $50. The oils and the organic lotions are exquisite, and they carry the whole Weleda and Burt's Bees lines, and basics like Tom's of Maine toothpaste.

There is always **Sephora** (555 Broadway bet. Prince and Spring Sts., 212-625-1309, various locations, check www.sephora.com for details). It's a great place to buy a mini eye shadow or nail polish for a last-minute date ($3–10). The Sephora brand line of cosmetics are actually decently formulated and come in a wide spectrum of colors.

Penny's Herb Company (E. 7th St. bet. 1st Ave. and Ave. A, 212-614-0716, by appointment only) is an herbal apothecary, aromatherapy center that does mail order worldwide. Particularly good if you have special health or dietary needs and are looking for an herbal solution rather than a chemical one.

auto

❊ 805 Washington Street bet. Horatio and
Gansevoort Streets
HOURS: Tu–Sat 12–7, Sun 12–6, closed Mon except in
the fall
PHONE: 212-229-2292
WEB: www.thisisauto.com

Auto is a high-end home boutique with a playful sensibility that caters to customers like the creative professionals who live in the neighborhood.

Unusual, fun, and colorful objects and decorations for the home abound at Auto. The young couple or parent will find much to be excited about here, from absurd objects like the Josh Owens piggy bank ($35) to Missoni throw pillows and hand towels (from $15). Other items include Eugenia Kim hats ($165–400), Subversive jewelry ($50 and up), and paper star lanterns. There is a reason New Yorkers sometimes have an entitled air. Auto presents a refreshingly low-key, worldly, eclectic mix of items for the home, from books to linens to curios. There are downtown brands mixed with high-end items, for the big baby in all New Yorkers.

You'll find the street is somewhat quiet, but it's interesting to speculate how this area became popular for stores—it is quite gritty, with old meatpacking factories and real live butchers still working nearby.

carry on tea and sympathy

❊ 108 Greenwich Avenue bet. 12th and 13th Streets
(opposite the entrance to Jane Street)
HOURS: Mon–Fri 11–10:30, Sat–Sun 9:30–10:30
PHONE: 212-807-8329

A typical English restaurant/shop that sells imported British fare and marketplace items for British ex-pats, Anglophiles, and everyone in between.

The restaurant serves such classics as Shepherd's Pie and, of course, all varieties of ultra-colonial English teas. This will be welcome news to resident Britishers, as they are always complaining about how Lipton tastes like dishwater. The shop, which has dark wood-paneled, neatly stocked shelves, feels like it should be in the countryside somewhere, and sells your favorite British groceries, chocolates, sweets, and teas alongside authentic teapots, mugs, and fun cards. They also carry their own line of T-shirts, as well as T-shirts devoted to the land of the Union Jack. The store does takeout and local deliveries, as well as worldwide shipping of their products. The store's matron will also dish you up a dose of cheeky British humor in keeping with the silly, campy series of English comedy movies the store is named for.

Tea Leaves

Teany (90 Rivington St. bet. Ludlow and Orchard Sts., Daily 9–12, they stop service at midnight and close at 1 a.m., 212-475-9190) was opened by music superstar Moby and his girlfriend. Both are vegetarian (Moby is a vegan) and the menu features breakfast snacks, salads, and sandwiches, of a vegan bent. Teany has a great afternoon tea special that includes a pot of tea, two of their yummy sandwiches, scone, and petit fours of the day ($16 for one, $25 for two). The menu is reasonably priced, and Teany offers a relaxed, unpretentious atmosphere.

Bodum Store and Café (413–415 W. 14th St. bet. 9th and 10th Aves., Mon–Sat 10–7, Sun 12–6, 212-367-9125). The French press is joined by a legion of housewares and home furnishings that smart of Scandinavian design tricks, at this spacious West Side store. Smart classroom curiosity meets housewares—you can dine on a light sandwich and dark, rich coffee or one of 100 types of teas, then shop for everything from a French press to an easel and pastels.

Tea and Tea (51 Mott St. bet. Pell and Bayard Sts. in Chinatown, Daily 11–11:30, 212-766-9889). A great little Chinese tapioca tea spot that is a must visit if you make it down to Chinatown. Taro, sesame black tea, and green tea milkshakes rock (with or without tapioca).

Up the street, **Aji Ichiban** (37 Mott St., Daily 10–8:30, 212-233-7650) is a munchies paradise! Meaning "very good" in Japanese, this snack shop chain stocks bins and bins of all the wasabi peas, jelly candies, and as many snack and candy varieties from across the Pacific as you can stand. It's a cheap movie date!

To The Market We Go

Flea markets are not casual outings in New York; they are a way of life. Many New Yorkers hit the flea market every Saturday as a part of their weekend routine. Here is a short guide to some of the best outdoor and indoor flea markets in the city. These markets are particularly good for finding reasonable secondhand clothing, shoes, and accessories.

Chelsea Flea Market (6th Ave. bet. 25th and 26th Sts., Sat–Sun 9–5). This is the grandmaster of flea markets in the city. Mingle with hipsters and creative types while browsing antique furniture, vintage jeans, furs, costume jewelry, linens, cameras, records, and assorted what have you. Every weekend, rain or shine, dealers from the tri-state (that's New York, New Jersey, and Connecticut) area converge in Chelsea to hawk their wares. Prices are steep by flea standards but be sure to haggle; if you come back at 5 p.m. chances are the dealer will give you a better price to avoid hauling the item back in his truck and to wherever he came from. Vintage Rolex Oyster watches start at $1200, mink coats at about $100. Other Chelsea Flea Market staples are African furniture and knickknacks, Tibetan jewelry, and art deco lamps. The section of the market on the east side of 6th Avenue at 25th Street charges a $1 entrance fee. Some vendors will ship internationally.

The Market in Nolita (268 Mulberry St. bet. E. Houston and Prince Streets, Sat all day). This market features young, up-and-coming, contemporary fashion and accessories designers selling their lines. It's worth stopping by if you are looking for something handmade or special.

Avenue A Flea Market (Ave. A at E. 10th St., Sat–Sun all day). This is a good flea market to find your Halloween costume or score a great leather jacket or pair of cowboy boots. The pickings can be slim depending on how late in the day you wander over.

upper west side

A classic New York neighborhood, the Upper West side is replete with some of New York's premier cultural institutions. Straddling the border between Harlem and midtown Manhattan, the Upper West Side is one of the most racially diverse neighborhoods in Manhattan. Lincoln Center and Julliard both lend a hand in drawing some of the most talented musicians, dancers, and artists from around the world who dot the Upper West Side's colorful avenues. Strolling along the wide avenues is comfortable, and nearby Central Park is a perfect place to take a break from shopping.

verve

✳ 282 Columbus Avenue bet. West 73rd and 74th Streets
HOURS: Mon–Sat 11–8, Sun 12–6
PHONE: 212-580-7150

At Verve, owner Steve Ginsberg has curated a choosy collection of handbags, shoes, and jewelry from all over the world.

Handbags are considered a status symbol, but you don't necessarily have to shop the designers just because you are in New York. Ginsberg has established himself as a connoisseur of accessories design. Ginsberg is a lecturer at the Fashion Institute of Technology, and acts as a willing consultant to many young designers who are trying to sell a line of accessories. He stays ahead of fashion, and it's nice to see this in a less trafficked shopping area.

Verve is a gallery of distinctive, colorful handbags, and no two designs are similar. Find eggplant-colored leather sacks; graphic-printed brocade and leather luggage; and elaborate, inventive, hand-worked details. Featured designers come from all over the world: Kooba (New York), Serpui Marie (Brazil), Isabella Fiore (California), and Orla Kiely (London), who makes vintage and travel-inspired reversible leather bags. Bags go anywhere from $40 into the hundreds, depending on size and designer. Jewelry designers include Citrine (Miami), Alessi (New York), and Wendy Mink (New York). Lorraine West, a favorite of singer Erykah Badu, is carried exclusively by Verve, and Annie R. is a Thai designer who makes lovely bent gold hoops. The jewelry ranges from $38–500 depending on the designer. (Also at 353 Bleecker St. bet. W. 10th and Charles Sts., Mon–Sat 11–8, Sun 12–6, 212-691-6516).

---

roslyn

❋ 276 Columbus Avenue at West 73rd Street
HOURS: Mon–Sun 11–7
PHONE: 212-496-5050

Eccentric veteran jewelry designer who knows jewelry design like the back of her hand and has great, timeless taste.

Roslyn is a jewelry designer—not affiliated with Steven Alan, her famous downtown retailing son. However, she's no slouch, having started designing jewelry at age seventeen. She worked with her boyfriend down on the Bowery, near the old Jewelry Exchange, whose recent closing she lamented as "the end of an era." No worries—Roslyn has moved on up, Jeffersons' style, to the relaxed environs of the Upper West Side, where her boutique luxuriously wraps around a corner on Columbus Avenue. "People here are warm, extremely creative people with great taste. I like to partner with my customers in designing jewelry. They have such great energy," she says.

Roslyn does custom design work. Each piece she makes is infused with her great style and philosophy; if Roslyn makes something you don't like, she doesn't hold you to it. She can re-personalize stones (from engagement rings to whatever) to fit a new context and meaning in a person's life. She finds inspiration in European, particularly French, jewelry design, and makes intricate, feminine pieces that can be worn all the time.

The store features over thiry-five hat and jewelry designers, as well as select antique pieces. The jewelry includes diamonds, semi-precious stones, and antique pieces. A few of Roslyn's favorites are Becky Kelso, Janine Pear, Xonya Ooten, and Jamie Joseph. Jewelry retails for anywhere from $65–500. She also sells vintage watches, which retail for between $300 and 800.

Hat styles run from wide brims to cloches to colorful rain hats by labels like Eugenia Kim, Misa Harada, Kelly Christy, and Jacqueline Lamont. There's a sporty handbag selection as well, by LeSportSac, Cammie Hill, Un Aprés Midi de Chien, and Herve Chapelier.

Roslyn's clients include a lot of mothers and daughters. However, she has stories about everyone from Elizabeth Taylor to Ed Sullivan to Ray Charles back in the day, to the likes of Yoko Ono and Ben Stiller today.

Nail Break

Now that everyone is getting their nails done—women, men, gay, straight—it is a good thing that New York City has the cheapest and best manicures and pedicures around. Whatever your reason for indulging, whether it's to finish off your look, show off new sandals, or just take a break from shopping, here are some of the best places in the city to get your nails done.

Dashing Diva Nail Spa (41 E. 8th St. at University Place, Sun–Wed 10–8, Thu–Sat 9–9, 212-673-9000). At this cozy nail spot, they serve martinis on Tuesdays! They are also open early and late, depending on when you have a hole in your busy schedule.

Go Girl (193 E. 4th St., Daily 11–8, 212-473-9973). Right next door to an East Village favorite, **Eugenia Kim Hats** (see p. 68), Go Girl is a laid-back nail salon where you can always find a chair and good conversation with the staff. One day a week, there is a special where you can get both a manicure and pedicure for $25—call the store for details.

Soho Nail (458 W. Broadway bet. Houston and Prince, 3rd floor, Mon–Sat 10–8, closed Sun, 212-475-6368). The women at Soho nail work hard for their money, providing all types of beauty services cheaper and faster than you can say "manicure/pedicure." Most waxing is under $30; a manicure/pedicure is $23. Call ahead for an appointment if you are going during peak hours (after work or on Saturday).

Rescue Beauty Lounge (8 Centre Market Place bet. Broome and Grand Sts., Tu–Fri 11–8, Sat–Sun 10–6, 212-431-0449, www.rescuebeauty.com). This is one of the most popular nail spas in Manhattan, and this location is out of the way and more relaxing and quiet than the others. They will serve you green tea, and scrub and soak your hands and feet with care. They use the popular line of Burt's Bee's products, which are superb, all-natural lotions and scrubs. Try Rescue's nail polish brand as well—they're high-quality and in rich colors. My favorite is Film Noir, a profound purple-red that looks stunning on most skin tones. In front of the shop are accessories and jewelry to go with your shiny new manicure/pedicure. For a full list of services, call one of the stores or consult the web site. (Also at 21 Cleveland Place bet. Spring and Kenmare, Mon–Fri 11–8, Sat 10–6, 212-431-3805 and 34 Gansevoort St. bet. Hudson and Greenwich, Tu–Fri 11–8, Sat–Sun 10–6, 212-206-6409).

Angel Feet (77 Perry St. bet. W. 4th and Bleecker Sts., Suite 1, Mon 10–9, Tu–Wed 1–9, Sat–Sun 10–8, 212-924-3576. A one-hour session is $70 and a half-hour is $40). Like its name, Angel Feet promises to take the client straight up to heaven, in less time. The spa offers reflexology treatments in an unhurried, relaxing fashion, taking only two clients at a time. The idea is to relax the whole body by working pressure points in the foot that correspond to every major muscle group and organ. Home and office calls can also be arranged.

upper east side

New York's Upper East Side is pristine and luxurious compared to the rest of the city. Some of the city's oldest and wealthiest residents live here—you can see screen shots from old movies if you peek up at the gorgeous building facades and in the windows of some almost ancestral homes. When you're done checking out Museum Mile along Fifth Avenue and taking a walk through Central Park, here are some great little shops to pop into. A bit further west, all along Fifth and Madison avenues, are flagship stores for every major fashion designer.

annika inez

✳ 243 East 78th Street bet. 2nd and 3rd Avenues
HOURS: Mon–Wed 11–7, Thu–Fri 12–8, Sat 11–7, closed Sun
PHONE: 212-717-9644
WEB: www.boebyannikainez.com

Delicate ethereal jewelry that takes its cue from history and fantasy.

Annika Inez is a cool Swede. So cool, in fact, she made the transition from interior designer to successful jeweler in less than five years. She looks like she stepped out of a James Bond movie—and her jewelry is so deceptively simple, you know a mastermind is behind all of it.

One of her signature items is a pair of hairline thin gold wire hoop earrings, with delicate chain clusters hanging ever so provocatively down the middle. One visit to her hole-in-the-wall shop and you'll be hooked. She takes the best elements of 1960s and '70s accessories—primary shapes and oddly colored beads—and floats them inside of her airy hoops.

Annika says the materials she uses are her major influence. "I mostly like vintage, because of the colors. Older manufactured pieces have cooler color." Check out the way gold offsets that very odd shade of '70s green, and you will see what she means. All of the jewelry is handmade using sterling silver and gold.

Other accessories she carries in the store are a line of decadent bags by Anjali Kumar (starting at $300), as well as the work of other local artisans. She carries lovely handmade scarves and a small selection of ponchos and sweaters. The lower priced items cost anywhere from $20 to $45—the larger, more intricate pieces go from $100 to $250. One piece she was working on was a large suede cuff overlaid with interlocking gold wire. Not surprisingly, her business is expanding to a downtown location by 2005, where she will have both a retail store and a showroom.

A Cocktail With a View

One of the greatest things about New York City is the vertical expanse of the landscape. Manhattan's skyline, immortalized in film and literature, is breathtaking. Walking around on the street, we very often forget that there is a sea of rooftops, where, perhaps, the city can be appreciated from an even more remarkable vantage point. And, even more so, after a hard day of shopping and with a fabulous cocktail in your hand.

The **Roof Garden Café** at the **Metropolitan Museum of Art** (1000 5th Ave. at 82nd St., Fri–Sat 10–8:30, Sun, Tu, Wed and Thu 10–4:30, closed Mon, 212-535-7710, www.metmuseum.org). If you weren't planning to go for the art (which I'm sure you were) you can enjoy a cocktail overlooking magical Central Park, with that profound skyline peeking up over the trees.

From the narrow terrace that runs along the outside of the rooftop restaurant at the **Beekman Tower** (3 Mitchell Place at 49th St. and 1st Ave., Daily 4–1 a.m., 212-355-7300), you have a spectacular view of midtown Manhattan. The atmosphere here is a bit on the stuffy side, but if you want to visit a hotel with some old-school flavor—think *The Sweet Smell of Success*, *The Big Clock*, and other classic Manhattan movies—this is a timeless New York joint.

A bit further downtown, overlooking Gramercy Park, is the **High Bar at the Gramercy Park Hotel** (2 Lexington Ave. at 21st St., opens at 4 p.m., 212-475-4320). The beautiful landscaped roof garden, a sanctuary from the street below, first opened in 1926, and the old-world feeling hasn't changed a bit.

Travel a bit west for a hipper, heavier scene at the **Hotel Gansevoort** (18 9th Ave. at W. 13th St., opens at 11 a.m., 212-206-6700) which, in the afternoons, say around 3 or 4 p.m., is a great place to catch a drink while watching the sun set over the Hudson. If you go after 6, chances are the bar will be overcrowded with well-heeled after-work drinkers.

sara

✻ 950 Lexington Avenue bet. East 69th and 70th Streets
HOURS: Mon–Fri 11–7, Sat 12–6
PHONE: 212-772-3243
WEB: www.saranyc.com

The silence is palpable as you step inside of this immaculate boutique, which showcases the finest handmade ceramic dinnerware, as well as other decorative items, for the home.

Naoki Uemura and his wife have been in this location for fifteen years, and he says that second and third generations of locals have returned time and again to Sara for their exquisite, one-of-a-kind wares. You could spend a good fifteen minutes examining the balance of a tilted bowl, or the perfect thickness of a handmade plate. Naoki buys pieces of art that speak to him. "I hear voices in a small piece of clay, and when they are noisy, I must have them," he says. You can find sets of tea services, single plates, bowls, and cups, as well as vases, urns, and much more, in a variety of ceramic styles, and finishes ranging from the very natural to fiery, sparkling glazes. Sleek, modern pieces sit next to naturalistic shapes that somehow beautifully retain the potter's handprint on their surfaces. Featured artists include Hanako Nakazato, who is a fourteenth generation potter from Japan, Malcolm Wright, Uko Morita, a Japanese ceramicist working in New York, and many others. Sara features some handblown glass pieces, as well as traditional wall-hanging vases from Japan. "We like high quality with a light price," Naoki says. You can find stunning pieces for as little as $30 here, perfect for a gift or an addition to your own collection. Check the web site for featured artists, as Uemura and his wife are always traveling and acquiring new works.

treasure chest

⁑ 49 East 78th Street bet. Madison and Park
Avenues, Apt. 2A
HOURS: Mon–Fri 10–6, Sat 12–6, closed Sun
PHONE: 212-585-3767

*The owner of this shop curates exotic clothing,
shoes, and objects from all over the world so that
chain-weary New York shoppers don't have to do
it themselves.*

The Upper East Side is well-suited to worldly, cosmopolitan
shoppers, as the boutiques from all over the world lining
its avenues can attest to. Roberta Freymann's tiny store is
almost too well hidden in its Upper East Side townhouse.
Intricately beaded belts, quilted silk jackets, embroidered
corset tops, and glam Moroccan sandals are among the
bounty you'll find here. This is just a sampling of the exquisite
items she procures on her jaunts to Thailand, Vietnam,
Argentina, Turkey, India, and beyond. For the past five years,
the Brit-born New Yorker has traveled the globe in search of
the prettiest, most wearable handmade garments on earth.
For a slightly more mature and sophisticated shopper,
Treasure Chest is expensive, but exquisite.

Made For You

As Manhattanites go through their daily lives, they have
precious moments during which they can express their
individuality—play lists in their I-pods as they whisk
through subway tunnels, milk with one sugar in morning coffee, desktop settings, and buttons on their jackets. In Manhattan, if you have the cash and the
wherewithal, you can reach the pinnacle of shopping

with the customized experience. In a city that prides itself on the unique experiences it offers, here are ways for you to explore your own personal style even further.

Abaete (560 Broadway bet. Spring and Prince Sts., Suite 306, 212-334-4755, www.abaete.com. Open by appointment only for custom and wholesale orders). Abaete is a solid women's collection filled with unusual and delicate details. The line was once swimwear only, and has since expanded to a full women's line. The clothing is feminine, made from silks, cotton toile, twills, and wools. Many of the fabrics have a bit of sheen to them, and gold detail is a signature characteristic of the line. The designs are playful but sophisticated, with details in a knotted neckline, a double-layer shredded skirt, or a graphic print. Swimsuit shapes nod to the designer's Brazilian roots, and the diverse collection includes several sophisticated maillots that recall tan starlets of the '70s. Tops range from $150–400, bottoms $100–300, and bathing suits are a little pricier at $180. Laura Poretzky, the founder and designer of Abaete, became interested in fashion design as an art student at the Rhode Island School of Design, and has done time in Ralph Lauren's ranks. She and her partner launched Abaete a year and a half ago to much success. Abaete is also sold at several multi-label stores, which are also great for finding the staples of each New York fashion season:

Kirna Zabete (96 Greene St. bet. Prince and Spring Sts., Mon–Sat 11–7, Sun 12–6, 212-941-9656) is a well-known destination for fashion.

The more popular **Barney's Co-op** (2 locations: 236 W. 18th St. bet. 7th and 8th Aves., Mon–Fri 11–8, Sat 11–7, Sun 12–6, 212-593-7800 and 116 Wooster St. bet. Prince and Spring Sts., Mon–Sat 11–7, Sun 12–6,

212-965-9964) caters to a younger customer, and has a vast selection of jeans to go with your Abaete top.

Linda Dresner (484 Park Ave. bet. E. 58th and E. 59th Sts., Mon–Sat 10–6, 212-308-3177) is a multi-label retailer from Chicago on the Upper East Side.

Jussara Lee (11 Little W. 12th St. bet. 9th Ave. and Washington St., Mon–Sat 11–7, Sun 12–7, 212-242-4128) custom makes suits, dresses, and more for the same price you'd pay if it were on the racks. Her Meatpacking boutique has a cold gallery feel to it, but if you ask her any questions, you will warm up to her, not to mention her beautiful clothes, quickly. It's simple—you choose from bolts and samples of luxury fabrics, pick one of her fabulous designs, have your measurements taken, then voilà! Signature items include minimalist sheer chiffon dresses and skirts, and it's guaranteed her pants will fit (as they are made for you!).

Bond No. 9 (9 Bond St. bet. Broadway and Lafayette, Mon–Fri 11–8, Sat 11–7, Sun 12–6, 212-228-1732). What could be more heavenly than a fragrance custom blended per your specifications? Owner Laurice Rahme has stocked her beautiful Noho store with a collection of twenty-two scents (and counting) blended to capture the personality of the New York places for which they are named. The most popular ready-to-wear fragrances are Chelsea Flowers and Eau de New York—others are called Little Italy, Madison Soiree, Riverside Drive, and So New York. Although she is French, she recently became an American citizen, and decided to give New Yorkers some great scents to call their own.

The fragrance specialists in the store will blend as many fragrances as you like in a two-ounce custom blend ($45 per fragrance) which you can house in Bond No. 9's specialty star-shaped perfume bottles ($40–150).

They will charge you about ten dollars less for a refill, and keep your fragrance recipe on file.

3 Custom Color Specialists (54 W. 22nd St. bet. 5th and 6th Aves., 3rd Floor, to book an appointment, 888.262.7714, www.threecustom.com). A visit to this Garment District lab is worth the hunt. Founders Trae Bodge and Chad Hayduk start each session with a quiz. What color are the veins in your wrist? Do you wear silver or gold? Do you burn or tan? The brightly colored products (all from an archive of color dating back to the 1920s) peek through minimal glass displays in this private, intimate studio. Experts blend colors on the premises.

Prices start with a $65 fee for the initial consultation with a color specialist and $105 if you want to meet one of the founders (the initial consultation fee can also be applied to any products you end up purchasing). Then there's about ninety minutes worth of mixing, fixing, and swirling until every tint is exactly right. Prices are $55 for two pots of lip gloss, $36.50 for eye shadow, $36.50 for bronzer, and $36.50 for concealer. Re-order discounts range from $5 to $10 off. Women who are having a hard time finding products to match their skin tone will adore the custom-blended concealers. Best of all, colors are never discontinued, and you can find hard-to-match colors that perhaps have been taken out of the current color lexicon.

The studio also offers bridal trials and makeup services, which cost $150 for two, $65 for each additional person. On-site bridal services can be arranged as well, with travel cost and time included in a quoted rate. They offer a 20-minute consultation at no fee for their ready-to-wear makeup.

Amore Pacific (114 Spring St. bet. Mercer and Greene, Mon–Fri 11–7, Thu til 8, Sat 10–7, Sun 12–6,

212-966-0400). Amore Pacific isn't exactly a spa. It's primarily a showcase for the luxury skin-care line of a major Korean cosmetics company, but it offers facials, bodywork, and reflexology. The store design is keyed to the five elements representing life's essential energies: water, fire, metal, earth, and tree. A four-ton basalt boulder stands in the middle of the floor. Thin strips of wood veneer crisscross the ceiling. Water flows over slate counters, rippling past products displayed like holy relics. As you approach, a description of each product materializes on a giant screen above it.

You sit with an advisor at a desk made of resin striated in several shades of red while you ponder a computer questionnaire about your skin that asks: Which of five flowers is truly you? The computer prints out your five-element analysis, revealing that you could use more tree. Passing through a curved lacquer door, you are greeted by a specialist who will administer a customized five-element healing facial massage. Ninety minutes later, you emerge with your complexion clearer and your elements in balance.

kitchen arts and letters

1435 Lexington bet. 93rd and 94th Streets
HOURS: Mon 1–6, Tu–Fri 10–6:30, Sat 11–6,
closed Sat in Summer
PHONE: 212-876-5550

Many chefs swear that this is the best cookbook store in the country, let alone New York.

Kitchen Arts and Letters carries nearly 13,000 titles on the subjects of food and wine, ranging from simple cookbooks to scientific and technical volumes on culinary history, sociology and anthropology, restaurant management, and many other areas, even extending to food-related fiction, organized by country and region. Included are many imported works in foreign languages—Spanish, German, and more than a thousand titles in French. Food is taking the main stage in American magazines and television, and as such we are becoming accustomed to an international language for cuisine and cooking. But at Kitchen Arts and Letters, you can even find books specific to region—for instance, South Indian cooking from the Indian state of Kerala, or regional Mexican cuisine. The small, one-room store has shelves floor to ceiling, where all the surfaces are covered with cookbooks. The staff is extremely helpful and very well versed in food literature.

The owner is Nach Waxman, a former book editor with deep ties to the food world. The clientele includes a substantial number of food professionals and the shop prides itself on its knowledgeable staff, many of whom have worked in the food industry, from bartenders to chefs to restaurateurs. Whether you are looking for Edward Dabner's charming book on the food of the Appalachian region or the excellent Gambero Rosso volume on Italian wines or Colette Rossant's book on the lost food of Egypt, this is the place to go. The store also deals extensively in out-of-print food books, including a free search service to meet customer needs and ships books anywhere in the world. Mr. Waxman will e-mail you an annotated new-arrivals list three times a year if you request it.

Kitchen-Happy

Because New York's restaurant community is so large and diverse, shoppers have access to the stores the chefs shop in. This is a short list of stores to visit if you are in the market for something special for the kitchen.

The **J. B. Prince Company** (36 E. 31st St. bet. Park and Madison Aves., 11th Floor, Mon–Fri 9–5, 212-683-3553) is a gallery stocked with everything from basic peppermills and strainers to more esoteric items, including quail egg cutters and a mechanism that cuts cucumbers and potatoes into cups, as well as tools usually seen only in professional kitchens such as sausage-making machines and baker's scales. The showroom is located on the 11th floor of a random office building, and can make a gadget addict out of any home cook. One of the best things about the store is the selection of knives. They stock Henkles, Wüstof, and Global lines. From Japan, they carry Misono knives (a company with a 750-year history and a descendant of one of Japan's greatest sword makers!), as well as Japanese Professional, MAC, Masahiro, and Bunmei. All of these knives are incredibly thin and sharp, great for fine slicing. The store also carries cleavers, saws, and various other tools for butchering. From the near-secret location to the business cards of every great restaurant/caterer in the city and country posted on bulletin boards flanking the doorway (all faithful customers), shopping at J. B. Prince makes you feel like you are a restaurant professional, or at least tight with one.

Broadway Panhandler (477 Broome St. bet. Greene and Wooster, Mon–Fri 10:30–7, Sat 11–7, Sun 11–6, 212-966-3434, www.broadwaypanhandler.com). This store sells everything for the home chef, a true one-stop shop. They have a wonderful selection of brands like AllClad and Krups, as well as all the coolest accessories you never knew you needed until now.

Korin (57 Warren St. bet. W. Broadway and Church St., Mon–Sat 10–6, 800-626-2172, www.korin.com) specializes in Asian eating accoutrement. If you've ever wanted to take home the sake set, the chopsticks, the plates, the bowls, or the bamboo steamers from a Japanese restaurant, a trip to Korin is essential. Korin is a restaurant supplier to hotels and restaurants worldwide, but you can also buy their beautiful porcelain tableware, and more, for your own home.

Bridge Kitchenware (214 E. 52nd St. bet. 2nd and 3rd Aves., Mon–Fri 9–5:30, Sat 10–4, 212-688-4220, www.bridgekitchenware.com) sells every kind of bakeware, cookware, and knife imaginable. Need that six-inch frying pan, or that saucepan that cooks the perfect amount of pasta for two? Look no further.

Bowery Kitchen Supply (460 W. 16th St. at 9th Ave., Mon–Sat 9–7, Sun 11–6, 212-376-4982). This commercial restaurant supplier brings a piece of the Bowery's kitchen supply district into the Chelsea Market, where tenants were handpicked by the Market's developer for their connection to food. Open for eight years, the owners specialize in commercial-grade, high-quality cookware, which despite looking old-fashioned and unwieldy at times, is just as good (and a heck of a lot cheaper) than cookware you will find at Williams Sonoma. Bowery Kitchen Supply also sells all kinds of gadgets for prepping food, including ones your grandmother may have used. They sell cutlery by the piece, which is useful. If you've seen a chef on TV using a gadget, or read about one recently, chances are you will find it here.

tribeca

Land of New York's wealthiest and arguably most tasteful citizens, Tribeca has become a destination for visitors and locals alike. The Tribeca Film Festival, Robert DeNiro, and other New York institutions call the neighborhood home. Tribeca is full of old printing houses and, today, many film production companies. The Soho and Tribeca Grand Hotels both boast beautiful bars and great music—and Battery Park is just a short bike ride away.

number (n)ine

✣ 431 Washington Street bet. Vestry and Desbrosses Streets
HOURS: Mon–Sat 1–7, closed Sun
PHONE: 212-431-4391
WEB: www.numberniners.com

Designer Takahiro Miyashitaq sells one of Japan's top men's brands in this hidden Tribeca boutique.

Number (N)ine is a lovely, haunting space with dark wood and intricately chosen hangings and lamps lingering in corners of the store—the room behind the swinging bookcase in a Bergman film. The main chandelier is from an old Morton Street townhouse, which has been oxidized by cigarette smoke. Two imposing metal doors in the back that lead to the offices were imported from Hungary, and the ceiling is made up of seventeen different patterned tin tiles from around the world. The clothing racks are made from gateposts, culminating in the designer's vision of a Transylvania-like store space.

create clothing that is approachable and unique. Pieces are not made in bulk to prevent counterfeiting in Japan, where the store frequently sells out of each item in a matter of hours. The designer has a strong point of view, and each piece in the collection is part of a theme. In 2005, red and black will abound, as will asymmetrical shapes. Leathers have been washed and wrinkled, and some pieces use wire to make them stand stiff. It sounds weirder than it actually is, but the customer here is definitely not afraid to take risks. Shoe styles include variations on sneakers, and lace boots with curled and pointed toes. Sleeveless jackets, long hooded sweatshirts, and kilts round out the imaginative collection. Accessories include black-on-black studded belts, bracelets, and cuffs.

The designer riffs on the androgyny of horror films and the gothic subculture, as well as the ever-changing boundary between street and formal wear. There is a strong punk and rockabilly influence on the collection. Most of the looks in this store are for the young, savvy, stylish man with some money to spend—most pieces are expensive to very expensive (from $300 to $10,000). A great place to buy a gift for a fashion forward friend or relative.

Button-up, Button-down

While New York hasn't quite caught up to the Savile Row standard of London, there are some good places to go find a shirt for a man for any occasion. A sartorially keen buddy of mine told me gravely, "Unfortunately, the dearth of good spots for shirts means that these are also on the pricier side." The upside is that when he dons a shirt or tie or suit from any of these places, he's guaranteed to turn heads. Oh, and each of these boutiques also does women's—but his are the reason to go!

Paul Smith (108 5th Ave., Mon–Sat 11–7, Thu 11–8, Sun 12–6, 212-627-9770). This classic British menswear designer is touted for his bold approach to fabric, pattern, and color, while sticking to old-world styling. Smith has also gone on to design accessories, housewares, and furniture. Prices for shirts start at $150.

At **Thomas Pink** (10 Columbus Circle, 212-823-9650; 1155 Ave. of the Americas, 212-840-9663; and 520 Madison Ave., 212-838-1928) the shirts sit prettily in their many suits of checkers, herringbones, stripes, and solids. It's a veritable forest of beautiful shirts, and the name says it all—British, cheeky, and slick. Shirts average $140, from casual to dress shirts.

Seize Sur Vingt (243 Elizabeth St., Mon–Sat 11–7, Sun 12–6, 212-343-0476). At this cool Nolita boutique, find two simple racks along either wall with great shirts that will make him feel like an international man of mystery. Fabrics are the specialty here, finely woven and in beautiful hues of every color. Shirts range from $140–160; pants from $250–300; and suits from $1,175–1,250.

Express Men's Store (584 Broadway bet. Prince and Houston Sts., Mon–Wed 10–8, Thu–Sat 10–9, Sun 11–7, 212-625-0685). This is a little-known treasure trove of lower-priced men's clothing. The shirting in particular is stylish and it's easy to stay on trend without dropping hundreds of dollars. In fact, most shirts here are modeled after Thomas Pink or Paul Smith, but no one needs to know that, right? Shirts are $49–78; ties are $34; suit separates are $98–300. You can look like a model without breaking your budget. (Also great along these lines: H&M and Zara.)

Ina (262 Mott St. bet. Prince and Houston Sts., Daily 12–7, 212-334-2210) is a consignment store that specializes in men's fashion (there is a women's store right around the corner at 21 Prince Street). Wares are in mint condition, and prices are reasonably slashed.

Odin (328 E. 11th St., 212-475-0666, www.odin-newyork.com). Odin's owners fluidly combine the best of street wear and tailored clothing for men, with a home and lifestyle element, including shaving, hair, and bath products (from Sharp's and Korress, among others), bags, art and photography books, pillows, skateboards, unisex jewelry, and much more. This small East Village store has been a quiet trendsetter, and could be what men in the city have been waiting for.

The giftables section has included limited-edition items from artists like Momoyo Torimitsu (cookie jars) and Dalek (skateboard decks), and the store plans to receive many more. Several limited-edition items that were first sold at Odin have ended up being retailed by larger stores, such as Salvor animal pillows, now at Paul Smith and the W Hotel. Other designers include Kim Jones, the womenswear designer who redesigned Umbro in the U.K.; Surface 2 Air, a New York-based accessories designer; Noah; Greige Manufacturing (who use vintage looms from Levi's to make their denim); Unis (who also has a shop in Nolita at 226 Elizabeth St. bet. Prince and Houston Sts., 212-431-5533); and Wings and Horns. T-shirts come from Pvblic and Salvor, while Oliver Spencer lends his excellent collection to round out the men's tailored items. Shirts cost around $135; pants around $175; and blazers and jackets start at $275.

south brooklyn
(prospect heights/clinton hill)

South Brooklyn has a slightly different vibe from its more widely known Brooklyn counterpart, Williamsburg. It is more residential and tree-lined. As such, shopping in this part of Brooklyn can be very relaxing, and the shops are set up to cater to a wandering customer, turning up on a random corner or in the middle of a block of houses. If you are a Manhattanite thinking about moving to the calm environs of Brooklyn, maybe a little shopping trip is what you need to start exploring this most excellent borough.

Nearby, there are other businesses popping up—a raw food restaurant, an excellent bike shop called Bicycle Station (560 Vanderbilt Ave. 718-638-0300), and an outpost of the popular Manhattan café Le Gamin (also on Vanderbilt Ave.), to name a few.

pieces of brooklyn

❊ 671 Vanderbilt Avenue at Park Place, Prospect Heights
HOURS: Mon by appt. only, Tu–Thu 11–7, Fri–Sat 11–8, Sun 11–6
PHONE: 718-857-7211
WEB: www.piecesofbklyn.com

A multi-label men and women's clothing store specializing in fashion-forward, up-and-coming labels that would be hard to find in a department store.

Owners Latisha and Colin Daring are a husband-wife styling and retail powerhouse who brought great fashion to this side of Brooklyn (the other side being Williamsburg). Pieces is located on an out-of-the-way street in Brooklyn, where you may ride past on your bike on your way to or from lovely Prospect Park. The designers at Pieces embody the hip, old-school vibe of the neighborhood. Most pieces are casual street wear or wear-to-work items that have been reworked and detailed with sassy, fun touches. Find, for instance, a pair of beautifully tailored trousers with a brightly colored ribbon sewn down the leg seam, or a high-necked blouse with a ruffled edge in neon green. The idea is to stylize fashion trends to reflect the aesthetic of young urban mavens, rather than fit the establishment dictated by runways. It's worth a trip just to check out how street style answers the bland cloned mannequins in department stores. Designers include R. Scott French, Sherri Bodell, Joe's Jeans, Anne Ferriday, True Couture, Private Circle, Anja Flint, Catch a Fire, Fillippa, By Caesar, Petra Barazza, Robert Graham, and Year Of. Clothes range from $30–500, depending on the item; average price for shoes is $150.

Also in Harlem (228 W. 135th St., 212-234-7425).

mcsweeney's storefront

❋ **429 7th Avenue bet. 14th and 15th Streets, Park Slope**
   HOURS: ?
   PHONE: ?
   WEB: www.mcsweeneys.net

A groundbreaking shop of a smattering of items.

Store "front" is apropos for this tiny space in Park Slope, Brooklyn, where *McSweeney's* literary journal editor Dave Eggers has opened a shop full of, well, not much you might want ordinarily. It is more a collection of abstract objects that he, or someone, finds very amusing and/or artful. The phone number is unlisted, the hours sign on the door is deliberately uncommunicative, yet the shop is genius. The store carries tiny dioramas, lumberjacking supplies, identical items with randomly assigned prices, models of bird feet cast in pewter, and excessive annotations from Eggers (see the introduction to his memoir, *A Heartbreaking Work of Staggering Genius*, for prep in this area). You may be able to locate copies of the acclaimed literary journal *McSweeney's*, which is sold nation-wide, elsewhere, but can you assess state fair-grade pump-kins at the same time?

sodafine

✳ 246 Dekalb Avenue bet. Vanderbilt and Clermont
Avenues, Clinton Hill
HOURS: Tu–Sat 12–8, Sun 12–6
PHONE: 718-230-3060
WEB: www.sodafine.com

Sodafine is an artist-run boutique that sells hand-made clothing, accessories, books, and magazines, as well as vintage clothing and accessories.

Sodafine manifests what is excellent about an up-and-coming area of Brooklyn (homes around here are selling for $1 million)—it is funky, colorful, diverse, and laid-back. Admittedly, this store is great for locals to wander into with a cup of coffee from **Tilly's** next door, but it's definitely worth the trip to Brooklyn to check out. The store specializes in handmade clothing and accessories, as well as books and magazines. The owners, Rebekah and Erin, relocated the store from Philadelphia in order to become part of a larger community of artists-cum-fashion designers, and vintage connoisseurs. Erin designs hand-knit and crocheted items under the name Purl-drop. Rebekah makes T-shirts and dresses, which she draws or silk-screens images onto. Other designers the shop features offer small and handmade items that are listed on Sodafine's web site. The colorful clothing inspires the imagination.

When the girls say everything is handmade, they mean it. "We don't accept designers who produce their goods in factories or corporate manufacturing facilities," Erin says. The shapes of the clothes and handbags are amorphous and contoured at the same time—hems and seams are not where they should be, and this off-kilter approach to fashion is what Sodafine is all about. However, most pieces in the store can be mixed and matched into a contemporary wardrobe. The girls wear handmade and vintage because it makes them feel good. Put it this way—you won't run into anyone else wearing the same thing you are. Vintage merchandise rounds out the handmade designs in the store. "Vintage has the same unique, one-of-a-kind feeling that our handmade items have," Erin explains. Shoe selection in the store is also excellent, vintage styles of pumps and boots from the '80s in particular ($20 and up).

Additionally, the magazines and books are documents of a youthful backlash to mainstream media—they are highly artistic and conscious pieces that cater to a broad range of interests, from art to politics to humor. "I like being able to offer a wide spectrum of artist-produced goods, which I think our customer is very interested in." The store carries comics, hand-bound blank books, and cards ($5–20).

Knitting

Knit New York (307 E. 14th St. bet. 1st and 2nd Aves., Daily 10–9, 212-387-0707, www.knitnewyork.com). This cool café is a soothing destination for tired urbanites of all ages seeking peace of mind. You'll find both the

Brooklyn designer and his mother hanging out here. You can get a full selection of coffee/espresso and tea beverages and baked goods with your skeins of beautiful yarns and knitting supplies. The café offers colorfully named knitting classes like "Sox and lox" (a brunch-time class on Sundays) and Ten Man Mondays (for men who want to learn this feminine craft in the company of other dudes). See the website for details.

A bit further south, in Soho, is **Purl** (137 Sullivan St. bet. Prince and Houston Sts., Mon–Fri 12–7, Sat–Sun 12–6, 212-420-8796, www.purlsoho.com). The owners have done a lot with this tiny space—a square table sits in the middle of the shop, and the walls are lined with cubbies filled with yarns from around the world. There is also an international selection of magazines and books to browse for more information on what's happening in the world of knitting, a pastime that's experiencing a resurgence among New Yorkers. The staff is knowledgeable and friendly. This is a great place to pick up the habit or to buy a gift for a special someone who loves to knit. Prices can be found on the web site, where the full catalog of the store is available for shipping (and photos of yarn detail).

Finding Fabrics

Treasure hunting in the Garment District in Manhattan can be fun, if you have some time to poke around. If you are looking for something special to spruce up your tiny studio apartment, like a new pillow cover or something more ambitious, like new curtains, a visit to West 38th and 39th Streets between 6th and 7th Avenues is in order. Located right around the corner from the Parsons

School of Design, you may see many student designers poking around the bolts of fabric. As there are hundreds of little shops to visit, it can be intimidating, but here is an introduction to a few of the best shops in the area, recommended by designers and stylists.

At **Fabrics Garden** (250 W. 39th St. bet. 7th and 8th Aves., Mon–Fri 9:30–7:30, Sat 10–7, Sun 12–5, 212-354-6193, www.fabricsgardenny.com) the vendors specialize in stretch fabrics, bridal fabrics, and reproductions of designer fabric (for instance, if there is a Prada skirt that is tie-dyed, they will have a version of the same fabric here). You should never pay too much, as the prices are always negotiable. An average price for fabric here is $5 per yard. Make sure you look closely at the bolts of fabrics before you buy because some of them have been sitting around the shop or in the sun and may have faded with time.

Another great store along these lines is **Neon Fabrics** (239 W. 39th St. bet. 7th and 8th Aves., Mon–Fri 9–7, Sat–Sun 10–6, 212-221-9705), which specializes in bright and neon colored fabrics.

A trip to **Leather Impact** (256 W. 38th St. bet. 7th and 8th Aves., Mon–Fri 9:30–5, 212-302-2332, www.leatherimpact.com) is a trip into a colorful tannery. The shop smells of fresh leather, and hundreds of felts line the tables and the walls in different colors. If you are trying to color match something, the salespeople will present you with at least three different options; an average skin costs $30 (depending on the size). They also sell rope and trimming, which is especially good for repairing a broken strap on a handbag, or for leather shoelaces. Leather Impact also carries embellished leathers, like laser-cut leather, and branded and designed leather.

williamsburg, brooklyn

On a sunny Monday afternoon in Williamsburg, people sip iced coffees and mosey down Bedford Avenue, toting paperbacks and dogs on leashes. The neighborhood is like an extension of the East Village in Manhattan, which is a ten-minute subway ride away, and during the day, it emulates the Village's lazy, meandering feeling. Ten years ago, many artists moved here and brought a live/work lifestyle to the neighborhood's vibe. Now many city commuters also live here, and on the weekend, it is as bustling as any neighborhood in Manhattan. Williamsburg is the kind of place where the day gets away from you while you are exploring the little shops, galleries, and cafés that line the industrial boulevards, all the way over to the East River. Many shops here are artist-run and eclectic, and are very laid back. It is a great neighborhood to find excellent vintage items, including furniture and clothing.

spacial etc.

✻ 199 Bedford Avenue at North 6th Street
HOURS: Mon–Sat 11–9, Sun 12–8
PHONE: 718-599-7962
WEB: www.spacialetc.com

Spacial combines lovely handmade works and cleverly packaged gift items, making it the best kind of travel store—the hip gift shop you wish you could find at a national park.

The storefront is prominent on Bedford Avenue, its large windows wrapped around the corner for over eight years. Spacial sells many items worth returning for, particularly the men's gift items: various shaving products, a wallet by the company J-fold ($40–60), and ultra-cool weathered, shiny handmade leather-worked men's key rings and watch bands by Billykirk ($40–200). Spacial also features handmade ponchos by Brooklyn Handknit ($180–400), and other local women's clothing designers. Mainstream brands like Jack Spade (bags, $100–300) and Camper (shoes, $135–250), as well as specialty designers like Sydwoq (shoes, $200–450) complement the arty-rugged vibe of the store. Costume and fine jewelry ranges from $12–450.

The store features minimalist installations by furniture designer Charles Rittman (www.onezerothree.com) that complement the store's naturalistic art works like the Peterman Bowls fashioned by a New England artist from a single piece of fallen wood ($100–400).

Furniture and Home Shopping in Williamsburg

Williamsburg has some great out-of-the-way spots to get new and used furniture, and most of these shops are located by the East River. Just ask a local on Bedford Avenue to point you in the direction of the water, if you can't see it already...

Two Jakes Used Office Furniture (320 Wythe Ave., Tu–Sun 11–7, closed Mon, 718-782-7780). If you've ever thought of refinishing an old piece of furniture but haven't, the Two Jakes have made a livelihood out of your procrastination. They collect old metal and wood office desks, chairs, and tables, and refinish them in a modern way. Stripped, minimal, and clean—if you don't like vintage furniture because it is too baroque, they've solved the problem for you. A bit on the pricey side but worth it if you can find the perfect piece for your office.

Desks and chairs range from $400–1000. They also accept donations.

Moon River Chattel (624 Grand St., Tu–Sat 12–7, Sun 12–5, closed Mon, 718-388-1121). This poetically named little shop seems as though it should be located in the Berkshires, but is actually tucked away on Grand Street near the waterfront. Moon River carries refurbished home furnishings and old-fashioned housewares: linens, dishes, kitchen items, tin toys, and an assortment of old-fashioned books. Many items are reproductions of old-fashioned objects found in the '40s and '50s, but some are originals. On your way out, treat yourself to a piece of penny candy from the selection on the counter or purchase a soda pop from an old-time fridge, or "icebox," as Mrs. Cleaver called it.

saved gallery of art and craft

❊ 82 Berry St. at North 9th Street
HOURS: Tu–Sun 1–8, closed Mon
PHONE: 718-388-5990

Art, furniture, and clothing gallery specializing in antique and modern home design with an Americana influence. Saved Gallery lures visitors in with its magical mix of old and new.

The Pacific Northwest sent Sean McNanney and Noel Hennessey to New York to save us from urban tunnel vision. They design clothing under the name Saved (also found at **Opening Ceremony** in Soho, pg. 37), and opened this offbeat shop and gallery space in Williamsburg to showcase their handiwork with home furnishings. Sean and Noel also own **St. Helen Café** (150 Wythe Ave. at N. 7th St., 718-302-1197) down the street where coffee is brewed to Pacific Northwest perfection. They meet several local artists at their café and show their artwork and handmade goods amidst exquisite antiques, as well as their own home designs.

At first, Saved seems like any other small-town antiques shop. However, antiques lend the context within which Sean and Noel design their own custom upholstery, handmade lampshades, silk screens, and other home furnishings. They work regularly with an antiques expert who also buys paintings and other pieces for the store. The overall result is an artfully arranged jumble of items that have subtle touches of modern design, playfulness, and humor. Located near the entrance to the store is a chair whose arms and back are carved from an ivory bone to resemble antlers, along with a matching ottoman. Both pieces are covered with Saved fabric: a graphic, black-silhouetted crest of a shield, axe, and bayonet are crossed as though ready for battle. A nearby chaise lounge has been re-covered in a fabric printed with flowers and birds on branches. The combination of modern, nature-inspired graphic design and found objects is what makes the store so interesting. "We like having beautiful antiques and a $10,000 table alongside a drawing from an artist who lives across the street that no one knows about," Sean says.

The Saved clothing line is mostly reconstructed T-shirts, thermals, vintage pieces, flannels, and kilts, which are silk-screened with natural imagery. If a lumberjack wandered into town for a rock show and beer—this is what he might wear. The store also sells handmade clothing and jewelry by In God We Trust and Bing Bang, two Brooklyn designers.

At the back of the store is a tattoo parlor. The tattoo shop evokes the solitude of a nineteenth-century artist or writer's studio—high-ceilinged, a bit creaky, with a floor-to-ceiling bookshelf containing esoteric works like Richard Feinman's *Six Easy Pieces*. Windows face a quiet concrete yard out back. Veteran in-house tattoo artist Scott Campbell specializes in custom designs that are influenced by both Japanese and antique art from advertisements.

mini mini market

✳ 218 Bedford Avenue at North 5th Street
HOURS: Mon–Fri 12–9, Sat–Sun 12–8
PHONE: 718-302-9337
WEB: www.miniminimarket.com

A one stop-shop to stock up on all your favorite '80s memorabilia, candy-colored clothing and accessories.

Growing up, my sister's bedroom was pink like a pill. Her dresser was a tall white chest with carved legs with gold painted detailing. An illustrated portrait of a little girl with big eyes, pre-Anime, hung on the wall. I spent hours in my sister's bedroom, reading books and magazines, eating candy, playing games, dressing up, and losing track of time. Mini Mini Market captures the essence of those hours by stocking all the fun pop '80s memorabilia reminiscent of the colors and clothes you see in Wes Anderson films. Located on an actual corner, Dana May Schwister and Ericka Louise Vala wanted to make their "market" a place where one could pick up anything from a birthday card to a candy bar to a small gift. They stock the store's walls and shelves with "things we loved from when we were ten, in the early '80s."

Schwister designs a popular jewelry line called Superfox and also carries the hard-to-find L.A. label Grey Ant that consists of futuristic-punk street clothing, such as high-necked jackets with elbow patches, varieties of cargo pants, and other deconstructed items. There is something to behold in every part of the store, including toys, visors, flip-flops, sunglasses, parasols, sundresses, T-shirts, stickers (yes, the kind you collected), dolls and pillows and dishes and jewelry and albums and stationery. The store carries about twenty pairs of shoes, featuring a couple of styles from the London brand Irregular Choice. The shoes come in fun rainbow colors that pop and have metallic insides. They even carry jellies.

Most smaller gift items are between $2–20; clothing ranges from $15–200; shoes go from $40–100; and jewelry costs around $30.

landing

❋ Wythe Avenue at North 3rd Street
HOURS: Mon–Sat 1–8, Sun 1–7
PHONE: 718-218-9449
WEB: www.landingbrooklyn.com

Former gallery space used to showcase the art of New York clothing and accessories design.

Landing is the size of an airplane hangar and as such provides the kind of shopping experience you can't have in Manhattan. The store is located on Wythe Avenue on the corner of the ground floor of an industrial building. Owner Lacy Vancourt has a fine art background, and as a result, she initially used the well-lit, ample space as a gallery. However, she became most interested in clothing and retail. "Working with a lot of younger designers who make one-off pieces is an art form in itself. I wanted to support that," she says. The space has evolved into a great intersection between Brooklyn and downtown Manhattan fashion designers. Besides Built by Wendy, a better-known New York brand, Landing also carries smaller Brooklyn-based designers. Artist M. Carter silk-screens his witty retro graphics (a six-pack of Schlitz, a gold medallion on a chain) onto surprisingly flattering apricot, pine, and mustard-colored straight-cut T-shirts. Air D, a line from Canada, creates super soft jersey tops that drape like butter. There are also charmingly modest pleated skirts, which feature a single, two-inch pleat along the knee-length hemline. A knockout item was a brown Ivana Helsinki topcoat printed with an original, cream-colored, interlocking block print tiled all over the body of the coat. Landing also carries many local jewelry designers, such as Le Petit Macho charm necklaces and bracelets, which are all one-of-a-kind. Clothing ranges from $20–100, coats are around $300, and jewelry costs between $20–60.

index of new york's 50 + best little shops (a to z)

index by shop type